General Eisenhower speaks to his troops in Europe.

President Eisenhower warns of the industrial-military complex that threatens the nation.

Private-citizen Eisenhower offers comments and advice from retirement.

Today Dwight D. Eisenhower remains the great voice of moderation whose advice and endorsement are sought by all Republican aspirants to the presidency.

In this book are more than 900 quotations of the only man in the past thirty-five years who has united his party, and led it to victory in a national election. These quotations cover hundreds of subjects, alphabetized for quick reference (with a complete index and biographical sketch).

Republicans looking for answers to party harmony and political victory will find them here in the quotations of the only official spokesman of the Republican Party. Historians, writers, students and all those interested in the man, his thoughts and his position, will find the information in:

and residing in Plainfield, Indiana

P9-DBJ-200

THE QUOTABLE DWIGHT D. EISENHOWER is one of six volumes of the quotations of America's foremost living political figures. The series, published by Droke House, includes: THE QUOTABLE HARRY S. TRUMAN, HUBERT H. HUMPHREY, ROBERT F. KENNEDY, RICHARD M. NIXON AND LYNDON B. JOHNSON.

Each book contains 750 to 1,000 quotations showing in his own words, where each of these political leaders stands on the important issues of today—as well as where he has stood in the past.

For 27 years, QUOTE, The Weekly Digest for public speakers has recorded a history of the times in the words of the men and women making that history. As a continuing service, the staff of QUOTE has worked with outstanding editors on this current series of political books.

THE
Quotable
DWIGHT D.
EISENHOWER

Compiled and Edited
by ELSIE GOLLAGHER
and the Staff of *Quote*

DROKE HOUSE, *Publishers*

ANDERSON, S. C.

Distributed by
GROSSET AND DUNLAP
51 Madison Avenue, New York, N. Y.

G. & D. No. 6709

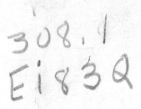
Library of Congress Catalog Card Number: 67–13265

Published by DROKE HOUSE, Publishers,
Anderson, S.C.

MANUFACTURED IN THE UNITED STATES OF AMERICA
FOR DROKE HOUSE, PUBLISHERS
BY
KINGSPORT PRESS, INC., KINGSPORT, TENN.
DESIGNED BY W. J. MC INTOSH

THE
Quotable
DWIGHT D. EISENHOWER

Contents

Introduction

Born in Texas, raised on a Kansas farm and educated at West Point, Dwight David Eisenhower became one of the most famous military leaders in world history.

Yet it was in the field of politics that he achieved his greatest fame—when he became the only man in thirty years to unite and lead the Republican Party to victory in national elections.

And eight years after his retirement to his Gettysburg farm Dwight D. Eisenhower still remains the great voice of moderation in American politics, as well as the only official spokesman for his party. His blessings are sought by all Republicans running for high office, and his advice is sought by successive Democratic Presidents.

"I Like Ike" was more than a campaign slogan for this Soldier-Statesman whose greatest interest was world peace; and he has been called "one of the most popular figures of the Western World."

The publishers feel that excerpts of Eisenhower's speeches —from addresses to his troops in Europe to his farewell address warning Americans of the changes of the industrial-military complex—plus his advice and comments since retirement, should be made easily available to the general public, both Republicans and Democrats. It has, therefore, been my privilege and pleasure to compile and edit this book of Eisenhower quotations.

ELSIE GOLLAGHER
1967

QUOTATIONS

··A··

ACCOMPLISHMENT

Our path in places is still obstructed by unfinished business, the debris of inequities and prejudices, not yet overcome. But, strong in the fundamental principles of American life, we have, in less than two centuries, accomplished more for the community of men than was won in the previous forty. (As President of Columbia University, speech delivered before American Bar Association, St. Louis, Mo., September 5, 1949).   [1

...America. There is nothing that the United States cannot do if every single man in it, capitalist and laborer, government and the people that are governed, put their hearts into that thing. (As Chief of Staff, Address before the Economic Club of New York, N. Y., November 20, 1946).   [2

ADENAUER, KONRAD

I think Mr. (Konrad) Adenauer has performed an absolutely indispensable task in the German Republic . . . He has oriented his people not only toward the West, politically,

but he has given them reasons for being so oriented . . .
He's really a sturdy man. (Appraising world leaders on
filmed television interview with CBS commentator Walter
Cronkite, February, 1962). [3

ADVICE

You cannot defrost a refrigerator with an ax. The only
safe way is to shut off the current, then let the forces of
nature do their work. (QUOTE, July 31, 1955, favorite
apothegm). [4

. . . **Political.** If I were giving a political piece of advice
to my associates in government, I would say, "When you're
in, never debate with an outer!" (QUOTE, November 5,
1961). [5

AFFAIRS

. . . **Military: Economic.** I have always firmly believed
that there is a great logic in the conduct of military affairs.
There is an equally great logic in economic affairs. If these
two logical disciplines can be wedded, it is then possible to
create a situation of maximum military strength within
economic capacities. (Speech at Press Conference, Washington, D. C., April 30, 1953). [6

AGGRESSION

Experience shows that indirect aggression rarely if ever
succeeds where there is reasonable security against direct
aggression. (Speech delivered to U. S. Congress, Washington, D. C., January 5, 1957). [7

We will never be an aggressor. We want adequate security. We want no more than adequacy. But we will accept nothing less. (Speech at Municipal Auditorium, Oklahoma City, Okla., November 13, 1957).   [8

History teaches that when powerful despots can gain something through aggression, they try, by the same methods, to gain more and more and more. (Speech over radio and television to the Nation, Washington, D. C., September 11, 1958).   [9

...Firmness. If the democracies had stood firm at the beginning, almost surely there would have been no World War. Instead they gave such an appearance of weakness and timidity that aggressive rulers were encouraged to over run one country after another. (Speech over radio and television to the Nation, Washington, D. C., September 11, 1958).   [10

AGREEMENT

For one who has had the task of helping to promote understanding among allies as they approached a military campaign and the battlefield, I have often wondered why it is so difficult for nations to reach any kind of accord in peace that they are forced to reach in war. (Speech delivered before 42nd Conference of the Interparliamentary Union, Washington, D. C., October 9, 1953).   [11

...Disagreement. The hallmark of freedom is the right to differ as well as the right to agree. (Speech delivered to members of the Senate and Commons, House of Commons

Chamber, Parliament Building, Ottawa, Canada, July 9, 1958). [12

AGRICULTURE

I stand behind . . . the price-support laws now on the books . . . to continue . . . the price supports on basic commodities at 90 per cent of parity . . . Farmers . . . would rather earn their fair share than have it as a Government handout. And a fair share is not merely 90 per cent of parity—but full parity. (As Republican Candidate for President, October 31, 1952). [13

Nature does not wait for the Government. You can't start farming by pushing buttons, and you cannot stop growing crops by throwing a switch. (Speech broadcast from Washington, D. C., April 16, 1956). [14

The country's prosperity cannot be sustained without a healthy and prosperous agriculture. (Speech broadcast from Washington, D. C., April 16, 1956). [15

If there ever was an issue that called for intelligence instead of prejudice, conviction instead of expediency, purpose instead of drifting, courage instead of timidity, that issue is the farm program. (Speech at Republican Women's National Conference, Washington, D. C., March 18, 1958). [16

AID

. . . **Giving; Receiving.** Giving aid is not easy, either for

6

those who give or for those who receive. (Speech at National War College, Washington, D. C., December 19, 1952). [17

AIRCRAFT

... **Modern.** Today three aircraft with modern weapons can practically duplicate the destructive power of all the 2,700 planes we unleashed in the great breakout attack from the Normandy beaches. (Speech broadcast from Washington, D. C., May 19, 1953).   [18

ALLIES

In the international realm, where we cannot stand alone, we have stout and loyal allies. Never write off even the least among them. (QUOTE, August 13, 1950, as President of Columbia University).   [19

Many of our allies are bound to us more by the loans which they have needed, than by a faith which our policies and practices should inspire. (As Republican Candidate for President, in speech at Cincinnati, Ohio, September 22, 1952).   [20

AMERICA

America is the greatest force that God has ever allowed to exist on His footstool. (Speech delivered over radio and television, Washington, D. C., April 5, 1954).   [21

Our country and its government have made mistakes— human mistakes. They have been of the head, not of the heart. And it is still true that the great concept of the dignity

7

of all men, alike created in the image of the Almighty, has been the compass by which we have tried and are trying to steer our course. (State of the Union Message, Washington, D. C., January 10, 1957).   [22

The basic question facing us today is more than mere survival—the military defense of national life and territory. It is the preservation of a way of life. We must meet the world challenge and at the same time permit no stagnation in America. Unless we progress, we regress. (QUOTE, January 18, 1959, State of the Union Message).   [23

In all history no nation has had a more honorable record in its dealings with other countries than has the U. S. The Philippines are independent today—by their own choice. Alaska and Hawaii are now proud partners in our federated, democratic enterprise—by their own choice. Puerto Rico is a commonwealth within the U. S. system—by its own choice. (QUOTE, February 28, 1960).   [24

... **Americans.** We are going to do everything possible to encourage every individual to exercise his own courage, to proceed to take risks if needed, but to go forward and to continue to build this United States into the thing it can be, something so free, so shining that I think none of our imaginations have yet even caught a glimmer of it. (Meeting with Republican leaders from seven states at Kansas City, Kans., August 21, 1952).   [25

... **Americans.** The things that make us proud to be Americans are of the soul and of the spirit. They are not the

8

jewels we wear, or the furs we buy, the houses we live in, the standard of living, even, that we have. All these things are wonderful to the esthetic and to the physical senses. But let us never forget that the deep things that are American are the soul and the spirit. (Speech after receiving the America's Democratic Legacy Award at annual dinner of the Anti-Defamation League of B'nai B'rith, Washington, D. C., November 23, 1953).   [26

... **Americans.** As this country was born in the self-sacrifice of its patriots, in their determination to work together, in their respect for one another—if we apply those principles today to ourselves at home, and to our tackling of our relationships with our friends abroad, we can dispel fear from our minds, and we can, as we achieve success, lead happy and full lives in perfect serenity and security. (Speech before U. S. Chamber of Commerce, May 2, 1955).   [27

... **Americans.** It's a habit of ours to set up straw men which we take pleasure in beating down. (Speech to American Society of Newspaper Editors and International Press Institute, Washington, D. C., April 17, 1958).   [28

... **Americans.** We Republicans see Mr. American in his high station as a free, self-reliant, proud individual. We are convinced that he can plan his own life and spend his own money better than some possibly benevolent bureaucrat can in his behalf. Any action that weakens any citizen's self-respect is wrong. (Speech at Republican Congressional testimonial dinner, Washington, D. C., June 1, 1961). [29

... **Americans.** America today is just as strong as it needs to be. America is the strongest nation in the world, and she will never be defeated or damaged seriously by anyone from the outside. Only Americans, only Americans can ever hurt us. (Speech at dedication ceremonies of Eisenhower Presidential Library in Abilene, Kans., May 1, 1962).   [30

... **Communism.** You can never cure malignant growth just by a hearty bedside manner! (As Republican Candidate for President, Milwaukee, Wis., October 3, 1952).   [31

... **Communism.** I equally wanted to emphasize this point: That when we go after corruption, Communism or anything else in our country, we do it in the American way. We respect every citizen in America. We respect his rights and privileges. We respect his equality before the law. If we do not do that, we endanger our own rights. (Speech at Duluth, Minn., October 4, 1952).   [32

... **Communism.** There is no other subject or purpose in which Americans are so completely united as in their opposition to communism. (Speech at Columbia University dinner of Alumni, Faculty Members and Friends of the University, New York, N. Y., May 31, 1954).   [33

... **Heritage.** We must walk ever in the knowledge that we are enriched by a heritage earned in the labor and sacrifice of our forbears that, for our children's children, we are trustees of a great republic and a time-tested political system;

10

that we prosper as a co-operating member of the family of nations. (State of the Union Message, Washington, D. C., January 5, 1956). [34

... **Image.** The image of America abroad is not improved when school children, through closing of some of our schools and through no fault of their own, are deprived of their opportunity for an education. (State of the Union Message, Washington, D. C., January 9, 1959). [35

... **Labor.** It is one of America's real marks of greatness that here a man from the ranks is not set apart. He has no class label. We are not a closed society. We are a society of free men, free citizens. We are all—by hand or brain, with skill and strength—workers. (As Republican Candidate for President, speech at Convention of the American Federation of Labor, New York, N. Y., September 17, 1952). [36

... **Russia.** The American people want to be friends with the Soviet peoples. There are no natural differences between our peoples or our nations. There are no territorial conflicts or commercial rivalries. Historically, our two countries have always been at peace. (Speech delivered at Geneva Conference, Geneva, Switzerland, July 18, 1955). [37

... **States.** Unless the United States is prosperous, unless it is strong, unless it is secure, there is no strength, there is no prosperity, there is no security for any state. (Speech delivered at forty-fifth Annual Governors' Conference, Seattle, Wash., August 4, 1953). [38

...States. The preservation of our states as vigorous powerful governmental entities is essential to permanent individual freedom and to national growth. (QUOTE, December 24, 1961, Address at Michigan's Constitutional Convention). [39

...Strength. Of all the free nations, our country is in many ways the richest and the strongest. Thus, there is imposed upon us a heavy share of the whole burden of free world security. Obviously we cannot help others unless we remain strong ourselves.—strong in spirit, strong in our economy and productivity, and strong in military might. (Speech delivered at American Legion Convention, Washington, D. C., August 30, 1954). [40

...United. America's policies abroad, to have any force, must be the reflection of the attitude and qualities displayed by our people. No individual, no group of individuals, however brilliant, however eloquent, can possibly do any effective work in leading the world toward peace, unless back of them is the mightiest force yet developed on God's footstool. And that is the force of a United America. (Speech to sixth National Assembly of the United Church Women, Atlantic City, N. J., October 6, 1953). [41

...World. I do not believe . . . that the United States can pick up the world on its economic, financial and military shoulders and carry it. (As General of the Army of the U. S., speech to Members of Congress, Library of Congress, Washington, D. C., February 1, 1951). [42

... World. In every country I hope to make widely known America's deepest desire—a world in which all nations may prosper in freedom, justice and peace, unmolested and unafraid. (QUOTE, December 13, 1959, in farewell speech on radio and television before 22,000 mile trip to eleven countries). [43

... World Leadership. Among the nations devoted to justice and freedom, destiny endows our own with the ability and capacity to assume leadership. We have the will; we have the means. Knowing this, an enemy of freedom would, in future war, fix upon us as his first and principal target. Thus on our security depends the existence and growth of a free world. (Address at American Legion Convention, New York, N. Y., August 29, 1947). [44

AMERICANS

Every American is a free member of a mighty partnership that has at its command all the pooled strength of Western Civilization—spiritual ideals, political experience, social purpose, scientific wealth, industrial prowess. There is no limit, other than our own resolve, to the temporal goals we set before ourselves—as free individuals joined in a team with our fellows; as a free nation in the community of nations. (As President of Columbia University, speech delivered at Commencement Exercises of Columbia University, New York, N. Y., June 1, 1949). [45

Today we are competing for men's hearts, and minds, and trust all over the world. In such a competition, what we are at home and what we do at home is even more important than what we say abroad. (Speech at Republican National Convention, San Francisco, Calif., August 23, 1956).   [46

... **Future.** Ours is a nation of men and women who have moved mountains, built great factories, tilled vast lands, harnessed mighty rivers and, in times of peril, have offered their lives for their country's sake. Our imaginations cannot comprehend what such resourceful men and women can and will do over future years, but our faith in them is complete. They will not, just as we will not, become slaves to class and mass, to so-called minorities, and to the use of divisive labels. (Speech at Republican Congressional Testimonial Dinner, Washington, D. C., June 1, 1961).   [47

... **Image.** As individuals we are frequently pictured abroad as rich, indifferent to all values other than money, careless of the rights of others and ignorant of the contributions others have made to the progress of western civilization. Undoubtedly these misconceptions are partially the result of Communist propaganda. But they flourish in the lack of comprehensive, truthful two-way information. (Speech to American Newspaper Publishers Association, New York, N. Y., April 22, 1954).   [48

APPEASEMENT
Realizing that common sense and common decency alike dictate the futility of appeasement, we shall never try to placate an aggressor by the false and wicked bargain of trading honor for security. Americans, indeed all free men,

remember that in the final choice a soldier's pack is not so heavy a burden as a prisoner's chains. (First Inaugural Address, January 20, 1953). [49

If history teaches anything, appeasement would make it more likely that we would have to fight a major war. (Speech over radio and television, Washington, D. C., September 11, 1958). [50

America is allergic to appeasement. There will be no appeasing Communist aggression while I am President. (Speech at Los Angeles, Calif., October 20, 1958). [51

All history has taught us the grim lesson that no nation has ever been successful in avoiding the terrors of war by refusing to defend its rights—by attempting to placate aggression. (Speech over radio and television, Washington, D. C., March 16, 1959). [52

APPRECIATION

... Small Towns. I think for any American who had the great and priceless privilege of being raised in a small town, there remains always with him nostalgic memories of those days. And the older he grows the more he senses what he owed to the simple honesty, the neighborliness, the integrity that he saw all around him, in those days, and took for granted, and that he learns to appreciate only as he grows older and dwells more in other places of the earth. (Speech delivered to the National Editorial Association, Washington, D. C., June 22, 1954). [53

ARGUMENT

Healthy argument over honest differences is always good. It's the essence of free government. It's the essence of democracy. (Farewell Press Conference in Paris, France, June 1952). [54

ARMAMENTS

...**Limitation.** A realistic limitation of armaments and an enduring, just peace remain our national goals; we maintain powerful military forces because there is no present alternative. They are forces designed for deterrent and defensive purposes, able instantly to strike back with destructive power in response to any attack. (State of the Union Message, January 6, 1955). [55

...**Limitation.** We must . . . encourage the efforts being made in the United Nations to limit armaments and to harness the atom to peaceful use. (State of the Union Message, January 6, 1955). [56

ARMED FORCES

I have seen the American proved on battlegrounds of Africa and Europe over which armies have been fighting for 2,000 years of recorded history. None of those battlefields has seen a more worthy soldier than the trained American. (Speech before Joint Session of Congress, June 18, 1945). [57

I feel that in our services we have today the best-educated group of military people that this world has seen. (Interview, December, 1952). [58

16

... **Career.** As long as I am above the ground I am never going to leave the Army. (As Chief of Staff, remarks at press and radio conference at the Pentagon, Washington, D. C., June 27, 1947).   [59

... **Discipline.** The day that discipline disappears from our (armed) forces, we will have no forces. (Press conference, Washington, D. C., May 23, 1956).   [60

... **Generals.** Don't ever become a general. If you become a general you just plain have too much to worry about. (QUOTE, June 20, 1965, advising a Young Army Reserve Lieutenant standing guard at World's Fair).   [61

... **Integration of.** A strong America is a trained and an integrated America. Nowhere is that integration more necessary than in our armed forces. We must not think, primarily, in terms of ground forces, naval forces, air forces. We must think in terms of coordinated action. Every consideration of efficiency, economy and progress in research demands the closest possible unity among all our fighting forces, all the way from bottom to top. (Speech at dinner of the American Legion National Commanders, Chicago, Ill., November 20, 1945).   [62

... **Military Men.** In a half century of national service, I have yet to meet the American military officer who viewed himself as a budding Napoleon, or even a Rasputin, and I suggest it is worthy of note that in recent world history the three major dictators, Hitler, Mussolini and Stalin, came from civil life. (Letter to Special Preparedness Subcommit-

tee of the Senate Committee on Armed Services, made
public January 23, 1962).   [63

...Pay. The military services are underpaid . . . We
cannot obtain and retain the necessary level of technical
proficiency unless officers and men, in sufficient numbers,
will make the armed services their careers. (Speech at Municipal Auditorium, Oklahoma City, Okla., November 13,
1957).   [64

...Respect. If we give the proper respect to our professional military people—if we think of them not only as
trained military men but as educated people, as patriotic and
dedicated and selfless as any citizens we can find, then their
opinions are of the utmost worth. (In interview, January 14,
1963).   [65

...Support of. Every man in the service is at his post to
uphold the tenets and ideals of American democracy. All of
them merit and need the intelligent interest and support of
every citizen. Otherwise, there can be no success in the great
program in which our Army plays such a critical role. The
servant cannot succeed except in the measure of the master's
will. It is the glory of the Army and its proudest boast that it
lives only to serve the nation. (Speech at Herald Tribune
Forum, New York, N. Y., October 30, 1946).   [66

...Unification. The Navy, the Air Force and the Army
must be one unit. If I had my way they all would be in the
same uniform. (Speech at West Point, June 20, 1945).   [67

ARMS

... Arms Race. Of all the problems confronting our country and its government today, none is more vital than that of finding a way to relieve mankind of the burden of devising, developing and maintaining arms which could lead to mankind's self-destruction. The burden is not only a danger to life itself, but, because of its ever-growing cost, an increasing threat to the economic well-being and security of everyone. (Letter to Ambassador James Wadsworth, March 3, 1958). [68

... Cost. Any survey of the free world's defense structure cannot fail to impart a feeling of regret that so much of our effort and resources must be devoted to armaments. (State of the Union Message, Washington, D. C., January 9, 1959). [69

... Defense. Our arms must be mighty, ready for instant action, so that no potential aggressor may be tempted to risk his own destruction. (Speech over radio and television, Washington, D. C., January 17, 1961). [70

... Peace. Arms alone can give the world no permanent peace, no confident security. Arms are solely for defense—to protect from violent assault what we already have. They are only a costly insurance. They cannot add to human progress. (Speech to American Society of Newspaper Editors, Washington, D. C., April 21, 1956). [71

... Science. In recent years the scientists have discovered methods of making weapons many, many times more destructive of opposing armed forces—but also of homes and industries and lives—than ever known or even imagined before. These same scientific discoveries have made much more complex the problems of limitation and control and reduction of armament. (Speech at Heads of Government Meeting, Geneva, Switzerland, July 21, 1955). [72

...Security.   Security based upon heavy armaments is a way of life that has been forced upon us and upon our Allies. We don't like it; in fact, we hate it. But so long as such an unmistakable, self-confirmed threat to our freedom exists, we will carry these burdens with dedication and determination. (Press conference, Washington, D. C., April 30, 1953). [73

ASIA

In the long run, Asia may become our most serious foreign problem. If Red China continues to develop destructive power, and remains dedicated to world revolution by naked force, then it is a problem that will have to be handled one of these days—and it is not going to be pleasant. (Interview, November, 1966). [74

ASSISTANCE

If I had to have any position of great responsibility in this country, there is nothing that I would allow to bar me from seeking access to the finest brains and experience that I could find on any subject of importance to us. (As Republican Candidate for President, Abilene, Kans., June 13, 1952). [75

ATOMIC AGE

I still hope earnestly that the Soviet Union may join in an

international effort to harness the atom for man's good. But I have such unlimited confidence in the creativeness of free minds and in the capacity of free men that I know we will, with or without the Soviets, achieve a more abundant life for those who join together in this venture. (QUOTE, June 19, 1955, outlining plan to offer nuclear reactors to free nations). [76

The known facts of atomic science remind us that the interests of the nations of this age are indivisible. Nations must unify their actions if this new-found power and knowledge are to create, not to destroy. (Speech made at the signing of the document ratifying U. S. membership in the International Atomic Energy Agency, July 29, 1957). [77

ATOMIC CONTROL

The international control of atomic energy and general and complete disarmament can no more be accomplished by rhetoric than can the economic development of newly independent countries. Both of these immense tasks facing mankind call for serious, painstaking, costly, laborious and nonpropaganda approaches. (Speech at Fifteenth General Assembly of the United Nations, New York, September 22, 1960). [78

ATOMIC WEAPONS

It is not enough to take this (atomic) weapon out of the hands of the soldiers. It must be put into the hands of those who will know how to strip its military casing and adapt it to the arts of peace. (Speech to General Assembly of the United Nations, December 8, 1953). [79

$\cdot \cdot \mathbf{B} \cdot \cdot$

BEHAVIOR

More than one man has found that in pushing too fast to get to the front, he has lost a following. (Speech at Republican Congressional Testimonial Dinner, Washington, D. C., June 1, 1961).   [80

BIGOTRY

...Hate.   There is no such thing as just a little bigotry; just a little hate. (As Republican Candidate for President, speech at Alfred E. Smith Memorial Foundation Dinner, New York, N. Y., October 16, 1952).   [81

BILL OF RIGHTS

So long as we govern our Nation by the letter and the spirit of the Bill of Rights, we can be sure that our Nation will grow in strength and wisdom and freedom. (Speech made at National Archives, Washington, D. C., at dedication of new shrine for the Declaration of Independence, the Constitution and the Bill of Rights, December 15, 1952).   [82

BIRTH CONTROL

If we ignore the plight of those unborn generations

which, because of our unreadiness to take corrective action in controlling population growth, will be denied any expectations beyond abject poverty and suffering, then history will rightly condemn us. (QUOTE, July 18, 1965).   [83

BOY SCOUTS

Self-development and service to others, independence and good citizenship, a sense of brotherhood and responsiveness to spiritual values—these qualities which scouting fosters mean much to America. (Boy Scout Week Message, February 6, 1955).   [84

BROTHERHOOD

Each race and each nation can learn from every other. There is none so close to self-sufficiency that it can do without the help and co-operation of others; none so primitive that it has not amassed a wisdom that can possibly enlighten even the most advanced. (As President of Columbia University, first of a Series of Lectures Dedicated to the Cause of International Peace, Columbia University, New York, N. Y., April 1950.)   [85

Without tolerance, without understanding for each other or without a spirit of brotherhood, we would soon cease to exist as a great nation. (QUOTE, January 30, 1955).   [86

If ever we were to lose our sense of brotherhood, of kinship with all free men, we would have entered upon our Nation's period of decline. (Speech over radio and television, Washington, D. C., May 21, 1957).   [87

The time has come when we must all live together for our mutual betterment or we shall all suffer harsh, possibly the final, penalty. (Remarks at Agriculture Fair, New Delhi, India, December 11, 1959).   [88

BUDGET

A balanced budget is an essential first measure in checking further depreciation in the buying power of the dollar. This is one of the critical steps to be taken to bring an end to planned inflation. Our purpose is to manage the Government's finances so as to help and not hinder each family in balancing its own budget. (State of the Union Message, February 2, 1953).   [89

The balancing of the Government's budget is critical simply because it can help every family in our land to balance its own budget. (Speech from Washington, D. C., August 6, 1953).   [90

Over the long term a balanced budget is one indispensable aid in keeping our economy and therefore our total security, strong and sound. (Speech at Municipal Auditorium, Oklahoma City, Okla., November 13, 1957).   [91

A balanced budget in itself is not a sacred word, but on the other hand it is not a bad word. (Remarks before National Association of Manufacturers, Washington, D. C., April 23, 1959).   [92

BUSINESS

... Politics.   I'm proud we have been called the party of business, but the businessman has to do a little bit of waking up . . . to the fact that politics means more to him than it used to. (Speech to some 60 top GOP Leaders and Candidates, Gettysburg, Pa., July, 1962).   [93

...Politics.   The businessman has got to make politics his first business because until we have sound government he is not going to have a prosperous business—not in the long run. (Speech at All-Republican Conference, Gettysburg, Pa., July, 1962).   [94

··C··

CANADA

Our two nations have lived as peaceful neighbors so long that in our own relationships we have totally forgotten the meaning of fears and lusts for conquest that bred the war from which we have just emerged. The ripeness of our friendship is apparent for all to see in a border which marks separate sovereignty, but binds together rather than divides. The secret is nothing other than mutual understanding and respect. (Address at Canadian Club luncheon, Ottawa, Canada, January 10, 1946). [95

Canada, rich in natural gifts, far richer in human character and genius, has earned the gratitude and the affectionate respect of all who cherish freedom and seek peace. (Speech to House of Commons, Ottawa, Canada, November 14, 1953). [96

Each of us possesses a distinctive national character and history. You won your independence by evolution, the United States by revolution. (Speech to members of Senate and House of Commons, Parliament Building, Ottawa, Canada, July 9, 1958). [97

26

...**America.** Our peoples move freely back and forth across a boundary that has known neither gun nor fortress in over a century. Our citizen-soldiers have three times fought together in the cause of freedom and today we are as one in our determination to defend our homelands. We have lived in peace with each other for nearly a century and a half. We cherish this record. (Speech at official opening of the St. Lawrence Seaway, Montreal, Canada, June 26, 1959). [98

CAPITALISM

We are flogging to death the horse (capitalism) that has carried us closer to our goals than we have been before. (QUOTE, January 7, 1950, as President of Columbia University). [99

CENSORSHIP

Censorship, in my opinion, is a stupid and shallow way of approaching the solution to any problem. Though sometimes necessary, as witness a professional and technical secret that may have a bearing upon the welfare and very safety of this country, we should be very careful in the way we apply it, beause in censorship always lurks the very great danger of working to the disadvantage of the American nation. (As President of Columbia University, speech at Associated Press luncheon, New York, N. Y., April 24, 1950). [100

Let us educate ourselves if we are going to run a free government. How many of you have read Marx or Stalin? (QUOTE, June 28, 1953, conference with newsmen on censorship and related subjects). [101

27

Don't join the book-burners . . . Don't be afraid to go in your library and read every book . . . How will we defeat communism unless we know what it teaches? We have got to fight it with something better. (QUOTE, June 14, 1953, address to graduates of Dartmouth College).   [102

We know that when censorship goes beyond the observance of common decency or the protection of the nation's obvious interests, it quickly becomes, for us, a deadly danger. It means conformity by compulsion in educational institutions; it means a controlled instead of a free press; it means the loss of human freedom. (Speech at Columbia University, New York, N. Y., May 31, 1954).   [103

CHANGE

In all things, change is the inexorable law of life. (State of the Union Message, January 5, 1956).   [104

Change based on principle is progress. Constant change without principle becomes chaos. (Speech at Republican National Convention, San Francisco, Calif., August 23, 1956).   [105

. . . **Leadership.** The product of change may be evil, unless leadership that guides it is broad enough to comprehend the general welfare of all nations. (As Chief of Staff, address at Annual Dinner of Wings Club, New York, N. Y., May 5, 1947).   [106

CHINA

. . . **Red.** The hope is that as a nation gains wealth, as it gets more consumer goods, then it tends to become more cautious, in order to protect its investment. Some say this has happened in Soviet Russia. This is possibly true. If Red China dedicates everything, not to developing the welfare of its own people but to a doctrine of world revolution by force, then it will be a serious problem. (News conference at Gettysburg, Pa., November, 1966).   [107

CHRISTMAS

Christmas symbolizes our deepest aspirations for peace and for good will among men . . . Peace is the right of every human being. (QUOTE, December 16, 1956).   [108

The spirit of Christmas helps bridge any differences among us. Faith and hope and charity are its universal countersigns. Peace and good will are its universal message. (Speech at lighting of National Christmas Tree, Washington, D. C., December 23, 1957).   [109

CHURCHILL, WINSTON S.

Out of your great experience, your great wisdom and your great courage, the free world yet has much to gain. We know that you will never be backward in bringing those qualities forward when we appeal to you for help, as all of us are bound to do. (QUOTE, April 10, 1955, to Winston Churchill on his retirement as British Prime Minister). [110

He (Winston Churchill) is a great man . . . He's a man who's a great thinker, and he's a great patriot, and he thinks not only just in terms of those little islands, or even only of the British Empire. He's talking about Western civilization

. . . He was a very great war leader. (Appraising world leaders on filmed television interview, February, 1962). [111

CITIZENSHIP

To blend, without coercion, the individual good and the common good is the essence of citizenship in a free country. This is truly an art whose principles must be learned. Like the other arts, perfection in its manifold details can never be attained. This makes it all the more necessary that its basic principles be understood in order that their application may keep pace with every change—natural, technological, social. (Speech delivered at installation as President of Columbia University, New York, N. Y., October 12, 1948). [112

America is exactly as strong as the initiative, courage, understanding, and loyalty of the individual citizen. (QUOTE, September 17, 1950, as President of Columbia University). [113

It is the firm duty of each of our free citizens and of every free citizen everywhere to place the cause of his country before the comfort, the convenience of himself. (First Inaugural Address, January 20, 1953). [114

. . . Equality. All of us who salute the flag, whatever our color or creed, or job or place of birth, are Americans entitled to the full rights and the full privileges of our citizenship. (Address to American Legion Convention, New York, N. Y., August 25, 1952). [115

CIVILIZATION

. . . Islam. Civilization owes to the Islamic world some of

its most important tools and achievements. From fundamental discoveries in medicine to the highest planes of astronomy, the Muslim genius has added much to the culture of all peoples. That genius has been a wellspring of science, commerce, and the arts, and has provided for all of us many lessons in courage and in hospitality. (Speech at ceremonies opening the Islamic Center, Washington, D. C., June 28, 1957). [116

CIVIL RIGHTS

My own belief is this: no true American, no American worthy of the name, would want deliberately to exclude another American from full opportunity to enjoy every guarantee under the Constitution. If he does there is something wrong and we must get at it. (As Candidate for Republican nomination for President, Speech at Detroit, Mich., June 14, 1952). [117

Wherever I have gone in this campaign, I have pledged the people of our country that, if elected, I will support the Constitution of the United States—the whole of it. And that means that I will support and seek to strengthen and extend to every American every right that the Constitution guarantees. (As Republican Candidate for President, Speech at Columbia, S. C., September 30, 1952). [118

Our civil and social rights form a central part of the heritage we are striving to defend on all fronts and with all our strength. I believe with all my heart that our vigilant guarding of these rights is a sacred obligation binding upon every citizen. To be true to one's own freedom is—in essence—to honor and respect the freedom of all others. (State of the Union Message, Washington, D. C., February 2, 1953).   [119

Mob rule cannot be allowed to override the decisions of the courts. At a time when we face a grave situation abroad because of the hatred that communism bears toward a system of government based on human rights, it would be difficult to exaggerate the harm that is being done to the prestige and influence, and indeed to the safety of our nation and the world. (QUOTE, September 29, 1957, addressing the nation on the Little Rock, Ark., desegregation issue).   [120

The situation calls for patience and forbearance. There are no revolutionary cures—they're evolutionary. (QUOTE, May 18, 1958, addressing National Newspaper Publishers Association, on civil rights issues).   [121

CO-EXISTENCE
The world comprises two great camps, grouped on the one side around dictatorships which subject the individual to absolute control and, on the other, democracy which provides him a free and unlimited horizon. In my view, conflicting political theories can exist peacefully in the same world provided there is no deliberate effort on the part of either to engage in unjust coercion or unwarranted interference against the other. But as long as deliberate aggression against the rights of free men and the existence of free government may be a part of the international picture, we must be prepared for whatever this may finally mean to us. (Address at American Legion Convention, New York, N. Y., August 29, 1947).   [122

Now, remember, the free nations have never said, "We cannot live with Communism in the world." It has been Communism that has said, "We cannot co-exist with free government." (As Supreme Commander of Allied Forces in Europe, informal press conference, Paris, France, January 12, 1952).   [123

This thing of co-existence . . . someone gets it and defines it with an adjective, and suddenly it is appeasement. Now, to my mind, co-existence is in effect—is, in fact—a state of our being as long as we are not attempting to destroy the other side. (Press conference, February 2, 1955).   [124

COLD WAR
There is but one sure way to avoid total war—and that is to win the cold war. (State of the Union Message, February 2, 1953).   [125

The only answer to a regime that wages total cold war is to wage total peace. (State of the Union Message, January 9, 1958).   [126

COMMERCE
Commerce here at home has made us what we are. (Speech before U. S. Chamber of Commerce, May 2, 1955).   [127

COMMON MARKET
Instead of talking about cutting each other down to the knees, we ought to co-ordinate our economic effort so the

Soviets will have to dance our tune for a change. (After a six-week tour of Europe, on the Common Market, September, 1962).   [128

COMMUNICATIONS

We are so tied together now with communications that, when a man has a bad temper in Moscow or in Bucharest or any other place in that region, we look at our reports to see whether it's going to have any effect before tomorrow morning. (Speech at Graduation Ceremonies at Foreign Service Institute, June 12, 1959).   [129

COMMUNISM

We face not only ruthless men, but also lies and misconceptions intended to rob us of our resolution and faith within, and of our friends throughout the world . . . To destroy human liberty and to control the world, the communists use every conceivable weapon: subversion, bribery, corruption, military attack. (Crusade for Freedom speech at Denver, Colorado, September 5, 1950).   [130

The demonstrated disregard of the Communists of their own pledges is one of the greatest obstacles to world success in substituting the rule of law for rule by force. (State of the Union Message, January 9, 1959).   [131

As long as the communist empire continues to seek world domination we shall have to face threats to the peace, of varying character and location. We have lived and will continue to live in a period where emergencies manufactured by the Soviets follow one another like beads on a string.

(Speech over radio and television, Washington, D. C., March 16, 1959).   [132

As long as the Communists insist that their aim is to dominate the world, we have no choice but to adopt measures that will prevent this from happening. (Remarks to Washington Conference of the Advertising Councils, Washington, D. C., April 13, 1959).   [133

We cannot win out against the Communist purpose to dominate the world by being timid, passive or apologetic when we are acting in our own and the free world's interests. (QUOTE, July 3, 1960).   [134

... **Aims.** We must not forget what the aims of communism have always been, announced by themselves: to divide the free world, to divide us among ourselves as the strongest nation of the free world, and, by the dividing, to confuse and eventually to conquer, to attain through those means their announced aim of world domination. (White House press conference, December 2, 1954).   [135

... **America.** The Communist leaders believe that, unless they destroy our system, their own subjects, gradually gaining an understanding of the blessings and opportunities of liberty, will repudiate communism and tear its dictators from their positions of power. (As President of Columbia University, speech at opening of Crusade for Freedom, Denver, Colo., September 4, 1950).   [136

... **Free World.** As of today the material and intellectual, spiritual, technical resources, professional resources available to the free world are so overwhelming as compared to what the Iron Curtain and the satellite countries have, that it is almost ridiculous for us to be talking in terms of fright and hysteria, which we often do. (As Allied Supreme Commander in Europe, to subcommittee of Senate Foreign Relations Committee in special hearing in Paris, France, July 9, 1951). [137

... **Free World.** Whenever communism attempts to over run any part of the world, the struggle there—whatever its fashion, propaganda, subversion, bribery, actual contest of arms is important to the whole free world. (News conference, Paris, France, January 22, 1952). [138

... **Free World.** The continued Communist menace gives the free nations of the world no reason for altering their course: to hope and work for the best; to arm and be ready for the worst. (QUOTE, May 24, 1953). [139

... **Free World.** It is not a struggle merely of economic theories, or forms of government, or of military power. At issue is the true nature of man. Either man is the creature whom the psalmist described as "a little lower than the angels" . . . or man is a soulless, animated machine to be enslaved, used and consumed by the state for its own glorification. It is, therefore, a struggle which goes to the roots of the human spirit, and its shadow falls across the long sweep of man's destiny. (QUOTE, January 16, 1955, on the struggle between free peoples and the Communist conspiracy). [140

... **Free World.** The spiritual, intellectual, and physical strength of people throughout the world will in the last analysis determine their willingness and their ability to resist communism. (State of the Union Message, January 9, 1959).   [141

... **Infiltration.** The . . . thing that we fear . . . is this idea of communist infiltration into our own country, into our government, into our schools, into our unions, into any of our facilities, any of our industries, wherever they may be and wherever those Communists could damage us. Now, it would be completely false to minimize the danger of this penetration. It does exist. We know some of them are here. (Speech delivered over radio and television, Washington, D. C., April 5, 1954).   [142

COMRADESHIP
There is a special comradeship that exists between men that have seen the sights of battlefields on a foreign shore. It is one that is never broken throughout the longest of lives. (As Republican Candidate for President, speech to Veterans of Foreign Wars, Los Angeles, Calif., August 5, 1952). [143

CONFIDENCE
Without confidence, constructive action is difficult—often impossible. With it, miracles can be performed. (Remarks made before 1959 Washington Conference of the Advertising Councils, Washington, D. C., April 13, 1959).   [144

... **Respect.** I never . . . discuss the details of communication between myself and heads of other governments, and for obvious reasons: because these people expect their communications, their confidence, to be respected, and I do. (News conference, April 3, 1957).   [145

CONGRESS

You know perfectly well that you just can't have one car with two drivers at the steering-wheel and expect to end up any place but in the ditch. (QUOTE, October 17, 1954, asking for a Republican Congress). [146

The Constitution entrusts the Executive with many functions, but the Congress—and the Congress alone—has the power of the purse. (State of the Union Message, January 9, 1959). [147

CONGRESSMEN

... **Religion.** A score of religious faiths, large and small, are represented in the membership of our present Congress, and it will interest you to know that a good many members of our Congress periodically meet together outside of legislative hours to consider how religious principles can be applied to the practical affairs of our government. (Speech delivered at the Assembly of the World Council of Churches, Evanston, Ill., August 19, 1954). [148

CO-OPERATION

No scientific progress can replace the virtues of co-operation, charity, patience and understanding. (As Chief of Staff, address at Annual Dinner of Wings Club, New York, N. Y., May 5, 1947). [149

It is not always necessary that people should think alike and believe alike before they can work together. (Speech delivered at Geneva Conference, Geneva, Switzerland, July 18, 1955). [150

Among equals, attempting to perform a difficult task, there is no substitute for co-operation. (Speech at Baylor University Commencement, Waco, Tex., May 25, 1956). [151

COURAGE

You can live happily if you have courage, because you are not fearing something that you can't help. You must have courage to look at all about you with honest eyes—above all, yourself. (Speech at Dartmouth College Commencement, Hanover, N. H., June 14, 1953). [152

CRIME

Crime is a real problem in this country, and it is getting worse. The problem is how to deal with criminals who are paroled or suspended. They are the ones who commit most of the serious crimes in the country. (News conference, Gettysburg, Pa., 1966). [153

We have got to punish people for excessive speeding, and killing other people on the streets and highways. Self-discipline is what we need. We must teach this across the board—in the press, in the schools, at home, in the churches, in Government. It must be some kind of movement. (News conference, Gettysburg, Pa., 1966). [154

... **Judges.** Judges have to give proper sentences, and not be subject to influence. I have come to the point where I do not believe in lifetime judges. I don't want to reduce their independence, but I don't think they should stay forever. (News conference, Gettysburg, Pa., 1966). [155

39

...Judges. With life expectancy getting into high figures, we have too many judges who have been sitting on the bench too long. This is serious, because there has been a trend toward rewriting the Constitution by a series of judicial decisions. (News conference, Gettysburg, Pa., 1966). [156

CRISES

A crisis is . . . the sharpest goad to the creative energies of men, particularly when they recognize it as a challenge to their every resource and move to meet it in faith, in thought, in courage. (Speech delivered at annual meeting of The Associated Press, New York, N. Y., April 25, 1955). [157

In our uneasy post-war world, crises are a recurrent international diet; their climaxes come and go. But so they have—in some degree—since the beginning of organized society. (Speech delivered at annual meeting of The Associated Press, New York, N. Y., April 25, 1955). [158

CURRENCY

When we begin to compare costs these days with those of the past, we make the mistake of just comparing moneybags. I sometimes wonder whether we shouldn't stop calling them dollars and call them dollarettes—so as to convey the idea we are not talking about the same thing we did in 1939. (Interview, December, 1952). [159

Government, no matter what its policies, cannot, of itself, make certain of the soundness of the dollar, that is, the stability of the purchasing power of the dollar in this country. There must be statesmanlike action, both by business and by labor. (News conference, June 26, 1957).   [160

No matter how much we like to say we can do anything we wish to do, let's not forget a sound currency is the first backstop of free enterprise. (QUOTE, May 4, 1961, at press conference, Gettysburg, Pa.).   [161

Our material strength rests on a free competitive enterprise, generating a steadily expanding economy measured always in a stable and respected currency, worth next month, next year, next decade what it is worth to-night. (Speech at Testimonial Dinner for Sen. Everett Dirksen, Chicago, Ill., September 16, 1961).   [162

No tax dollar, even though it is wisely spent by bureaucrats sitting down in Washington, can possibly bring with it that great, human individual concern which means so much to all of us. Any private dollar is worth four government dollars. (QUOTE, November 26, 1961).   [163

·· D ··

DEALS

I have heard of all kinds of deals, all of us have, they have borne many adjectives in this country over the past twenty years—I'm strictly a no-deal man. (As Candidate for Republican nomination for President, Detroit, Mich., June 14, 1952).   [164

DEBATE

Ours would be a sickly democracy—sluggish with age and complacence—if we did not debate great issues with honest zeal. Any enemy that professes to find comfort in this fact confesses his ignorance of democracy's true strength. (As Republican Candidate for President, speech at the Alfred E. Smith Memorial Foundation Dinner, New York, N. Y., October 16, 1952).   [165

If the day comes when personal conflicts are more significant than honest debate on great policy, then the flame of freedom will flicker low indeed. (Speech to American Newspaper Publishers Association, New York, N. Y., April 22, 1954).   [166

Without exhaustive debate—even heated debate—of ideas and programs, free government would weaken and wither. (Speech at Columbia University, New York, N. Y., May 31, 1954). [167

DEBTS

I shall not be a party to reckless spending schemes which would increase the burden of debt of our grandchildren, by resuming, in prosperous times, the practice of deficit financing. (Message to Congress, Washington, D. C., August 8, 1960). [168

If the (President John F. Kennedy) knows what's good for us, we'll pay our debts as we go along. (Commenting on his successor, Palm Springs, Calif., February 8, 1961). [169

DECISIONS

Men are not gods. They are not going to be Olympian in their judgments, and they are not going to be fully guided by qualities of mercy and justice and right in making their decisions. They are going to try to decide, "What is good for me?" (As Allied Supreme Commander in Europe, views given to subcommittee of Senate Foreign Relations Committee in special hearing, Paris, France, July 9, 1951). [170

They (Joint Chiefs of Staff) are entitled to their opinions, but I have to make the decisions. (Press conference, February 2, 1955). [171

DECLARATION OF INDEPENDENCE

The Constitution and the Declaration can live only as long as they are enshrined in our hearts and minds. If they are not so enshrined, they would be no better than mummies in their glass cases, and they could in time become idols

43

whose worship would be a grim mockery of the true faith. Only as these documents are reflected in the thoughts and acts of Americans can they remain symbols of a power that can move the world. (Speech at National Archives, Washington, D. C., December 15, 1952).   [172

We venerate more widely than any other document, except only the Bible, the American Declaration of Independence. That declaration was more than a call to national action. It is a voice of conscience establishing clear, enduring values applicable to the lives of all men. (Speech over radio and television, Washington, D. C., September 10, 1959).   [173

Everyone young and old, might take time to ponder the first two paragraphs given to us by founders of our nation in 1776. (Remarks on Independence Day observance, July 3, 1963).   [174

DEFAMATION
In this country, if someone dislikes you, or accuses you, he must come up in front. He cannot hide behind the shadow. He cannot assassinate you or your character from behind, without suffering the penalties an outraged citizenry will impose. (Speech after receiving the America's Democratic Legacy Award at Annual Dinner of the Anti-Defamation League of B'nai B'rith, Washington, D. C., November 23, 1953).   [175

DEFENSE
Nobody can defend another nation. The true defense of a nation must be found in its own soul, and you cannot import

a soul. (As General of the Army, speech to Members of Congress, Washington, D. C., February 1, 1951).   [176

We know that in the long run no nation can be defended from without. Rome tried it and built walls. Other nations have tried it. (As Allied Supreme Commander in Europe, views given to subcommittee of Senate Foreign Relations Committee in special hearing, Paris, France, July 9, 1951).   [177

The problem in defense is how far you can go without destroying from within what you are trying to defend from without. (QUOTE, January 18, 1953).   [178

We must be ready to dare all for our country. For history does not long entrust the care of freedom to the weak or the timid. We must acquire proficiency in defense and display stamina in purpose. (First Inaugural Address, January 20, 1953).   [179

A true posture of defense is composed of three factors—spiritual, military and economic. (Press conference, Washington, D. C., April 30, 1953).   [180

No matter how crushing a blow we strike in retaliation for an attack upon us, to permit our great centers of population and industry to lie exposed to the weapons of modern war is to invite both an attack and a national catastrophe. (QUOTE, July 22, 1956).   [181

As to our security, the spiritual powers of a nation—its underlying religious faith, its self-reliance, its capacity for intelligent sacrifice—these are the most important stones in any defense structure. (Speech over radio and television, Washington, D. C., November 7, 1957). [182

Paraphrasing an American patriot, our motto must be: "Billions for defense; not one cent for needless waste." (Speech to American Society of Newspaper Editors and International Press Institute, Washington, D. C., April 17, 1958). [183

... **Budget.** For myself, I have seen unwise military cuts before. I have seen their terrible consequences. I am determined to do all I can to see that we do not follow that foolhardy road again. (QUOTE, May 19, 1957, in radio and television address). [184

... **Budget.** I personally believe—with I am sure very little company in either party—that the defense budget should be substantially reduced. (QUOTE, July 1, 1962). [185

... **Cost.** We must be fearful that we do not prove that free countries can be defended only at the cost of bankruptcy. (QUOTE, April 6, 1952). [186

... **Definition of.** Military defense is made up of many things. The things that defend the nation or that act for it on the field of battle are many and varied, and as complex as the nation itself. The fighting forces are but the cutting edge of a very great machine, the inspiration and the power for which are found in the hearts of the citizens. All of our various mechanisms that are necessary are represented in our industrial capacity, our economic processes, and so on, so that when we talk about defending the free world we are not merely talking about defense in the terms of divisions and battleships and planes. We are talking about what is in our hearts, what we understand with our heads, and what we are going to do as a body. (As General of the Army, speech to Members of Congress, February 1, 1951).   [187

DE GAULLE, CHARLES

You (de Gaulle) yourself have come to symbolize for us not only French valor and resolution in the face of adversity but also a dynamic and youthful France determined to go forward with renewed vigor and faith. (Letter congratulating Gen. de Gaulle upon his inauguration, January 9, 1959).   [188

When he (Charles de Gaulle) disagrees with you, he's a difficult one—there's no question—he knows it. But he and I, in all these years, and we've had some very tough arguments, both in war and since, but I'm sure it's one of those cases where we've never lost our respect for each other, and indeed, our affection. I like him! (Television interview with CBS commentator Walter Cronkite, February, 1962). [189

All the world knows he (Charles de Gaulle) can be difficult and obstinate, and also he's often right. He was always very touchy during the war . . . because although he felt he was Louis XIV, he knew I could cut off his rations and equipment. But we always managed to get on . . . Foster Dulles and I decided way back in the '50s that de

Gaulle was the only man who could save France. So we did what we could, mainly by talking to French people who came to Washington and telling them what a good job we thought he could do. So I was delighted when de Gaulle got back to power, even though I don't agree with all his ideas. (Interview, August, 1962).   [190

DEMOCRACY

The American system rests upon the rights and dignity of the individual. The success of that system depends upon the assumption by each one of personal, individual responsibility for the safety and welfare of the whole. No government official, no soldier, be he brass hat or pfc., no other person can assume your responsibilities—else democracy will cease to exist. (Address at American Legion Convention, New York, N. Y., August 29, 1947).   [191

Our aim—to which we must be pledged in joyous, generous and confident dedication—is ever clear, ever the same. It is the idea of human freedom—that glorious gift of our Judeo-Christian traditions. This idea—democracy—is not a mere sentimental mood, nor some casually inherited persuasion. It is a doctrine of life and a definition of man. (As Republican Candidate for President, speech at Alfred E. Smith Memorial Foundation dinner, New York, N. Y., October 16, 1952).   [192

... Dictatorship. Never let any man for one second forget his own responsibility to support, defend, the idea that eventually justice and right can supplant dictatorship and force. (Speech to Chamber of Commerce of the State of New York, New York City, May 7, 1948).   [193

... Socialism.   We believe that our free and socially responsible enterprise has demonstrated definite advantages over an economy based upon a socialistic pattern of organization. But we do recognize that those nations whose particular problems lead them to adopt a socialist economy should not be condemned for doing so. (Address before Commonwealth Club of California, San Francisco, Calif., October 20, 1960).   [194

DESPOTISM
Despotism, whatever its guise, develops when men, losing faith in themselves, surrender bit by bit their responsibilities to a central authority. (QUOTE, November 26, 1950, as President of Columbia University).   [195

DETERMINATION
A business, an industry, the nation itself, prospers and is strong only insofar as its men and women are determined to make it great and work together for that end. (As Chief of Staff, Address before the National Board of Fire Underwriters, New York, N. Y., May 27, 1947).   [196

... Foreign Affairs.   If we will dedicate our minds to worthy purposes, lift up our hearts in determination that it shall be done, there is no foreign power that can challenge us. There is no task in the foreign field that can defeat our leadership, our efforts to make it strong to serve our interests

49

and the interests of others in the free world. (As Republican Candidate for President, speech to Veterans of Foreign Wars, Los Angeles, Calif., August 5, 1952).   [197

DICTATORS

No dictator is ever as free to do exactly as he wants as the world seems to think. A dictator has the problem of public opinion—how public opinion may be forced through the police state . . . He couldn't possibly just have 200 million Russians hating him and wanting to kill him, including the Army and everything else. There would be no dictator. He wouldn't be there. So, he has his problems, too . . . We must not make the mistake of saying that everything he does we think is evil is entirely of his own volition. (Comments on a CBS television broadcast, February 15, 1962).   [198

DICTATORSHIPS

I believe myself that, if we can keep a sturdy course and a steady course, firm in what we believe to be right, that finally even the Soviets begin to learn that it is not to their benefit to go in and try to buy, bribe and subvert generally people that are themselves trying to live their own lives; because, finally, what all history shows, that, when any dictatorship goes too far in its control, finally, whether it be the Roman Empire or Genghis Khan's or Napoleon's or anyone's else, just the very size of the thing begins to defeat them. (News conference, August 20, 1958).   [199

... **Democracies.** The real strength with which the self-governing democracies have met the tests of history is something denied to dictatorships. It is found in the quality of our life, and the vigor of our ideals. (Speech at Municipal Auditorium, Oklahoma City, Okla., November 13, 1957). [200

DIFFERENCES

... **Allies.** When we occasionally differ with some allies, we are, as a free people, simply being true both to ourselves and to our common cause. (As Presidential Nominee, speech delivered over radio and television, Washington, D. C., September 19, 1956). [201

DIFFICULTIES

... **Success.** Difficulties are often of such slight substance that they fade into nothing at the first sign of success. (As Supreme Commander, Europe, speech delivered before the English Speaking Union, London, England, July 3, 1951). [202

DIPLOMACY

We must put effort, skill and faith in our diplomacy . . . for upon it, ultimately, will depend the prevention of World War III. (Speech delivered over radio and television, Washington, D. C., September 19, 1956). [203

We need more individual diplomats from Main Street, from our farms, schools, laboratories—from every walk of life. People-to-people diplomacy means thousands of part-time ambassadors—all working for better relationships among all peoples. (Remarks before Third National Conference on Exchange of Persons, Washington, D. C., January 30, 1959). [204

DIPLOMATS

... **Duties of.** This is what we expect our diplomats to do—to be officers of the great army that has as its first business the developing and sustaining of a peace with justice and with honor. (Speech at Ceremonies Dedicating Edmund A. Walsh School of Foreign Service, Georgetown University, Washington, D. C., October 13, 1958).   [205

DISARMAMENT

No nation can live in the true spirit of peace . . . until the trend toward increasingly destructive armaments is reversed. (QUOTE, July 29, 1956, Interview).   [206

The world cannot afford to stand still on disarmament. We must never give up the search for a basis of agreement. (State of the Union Message, January 9, 1958).   [207

Men everywhere want to disarm. They want their wealth and labor to be spent not for war, but for food, for clothing, for shelter, for medicine, for schools. (Speech delivered at Fifteenth General Assembly of United Nations, New York, N. Y., September 22, 1960).   [208

... **Imperative.** Controlled, universal disarmament is the imperative of our time. The demand for it by the hundreds of millions whose chief concern is the long future of themselves and their children will, I hope, become so universal and so insistent that no man, no government anywhere, can withstand it. (Address to Indian Parliament, New Delhi, India, December 10, 1959).   [209

... Inspection. A disarmament program which was not inspected and guaranteed would increase, not reduce, the risk of war. (Speech delivered at Fifteenth General Assembly of the United Nations, New York, N. Y., September 22, 1960).   [210

DISCOVERIES

The world will witness future discoveries even more startling than that of nuclear fission. The question is: Will we be the ones to make them. (Speech at Municipal Auditorium, Oklahoma City, Okla., November 13, 1957).   [211

DISCRIMINATION

We must strive to have every person judged and measured by what he is, rather than by his color, race or religion. (State of the Union Message, January 5, 1956).   [212

DISCUSSION

There is no future for progress and civilization unless the conference table supplants the battleground as the arbiter of disputes. (Speech delivered before 42nd Conference of the Interparliamentary Union, Washington, D. C., October 9, 1953).   [213

If people are to be true partners, if nations are to make partnerships a real success, we must be careful to represent to the best of our ability both sides of an argument, because in so doing we remove bitterness. We may be disappointed that our friend does not see with the same clarity that we think we see the particular elements of a problem, but, if we are careful to explain both sides, we will always settle them in a spirit of conciliation and in partnership and not of contestants in a lawsuit or any other kind of contest. (Speech delivered before 13th Annual Meeting of the Inter-American Press Association, Washington, D. C., October 16, 1957).   [214

DOUBT

Show me anything that's been remembered by man in the world, that has been accomplished by the doubters or the people who said "No." (Press conference, Paris, France, June, 1952).   [215

DULLES, JOHN FOSTER

You (John Foster Dulles) have been a staunch bulwark of our nation against the machinations of imperialistic Communism. (On Mr. Dulles' resignation as Secretary of State, April 16, 1959).   [216

From his (John Foster Dulles) life and work, humanity will, in the years to come, gain renewed inspiration to work ever harder for the attainment of the goal of peace with justice. In the pursuit of that goal, he ignored every personal cost and sacrifice, however great. (Speech paying tribute to John Foster Dulles, May 24, 1959).   [217

· · E · ·

EAST AND WEST

We must never be deluded into believing that one week
of friendly, even fruitful, negotiation can wholly eliminate a
problem arising out of the wide gulf that separates, so far,
East and West—a gulf so wide and deep as the differences
between individual liberty and regimentation, as wide and
deep as the gulf that lies between the concept of man made
in the image of his God and the concept of man as a mere
instrument of the state. (Speech over radio and television,
Washington, D. C., July 25, 1955).   [218

ECONOMY

Ours is the most dynamic economy yet devised by man, a
progress-sharing economy whose advance benefits every
man, woman and child living within it. (Speech at annual
meeting of The Associated Press, New York, N. Y., April
25, 1955).   [219

I think the Federal Government should not disturb the
economy of our country except when it has to. (Press conference, February 6, 1957).   [220

One truth we should always hold before our eyes: Reckless expenditure in the name of economic stimulation is both wrong and self-defeating. (Speech to American Management Association, New York City, May 20, 1958).   [221

... **Definition.** Our economy is not the Federal Reserve System, or the Treasury, or the Congress, or the White House. This nation of 43 million families, 174 million people—what we all think and what we do—that is our economy. (Speech to the Economic Mobilization Conference conducted by the American Management Association, New York City, May 20, 1958).   [222

... **Free.** I still believe the free economy is a better way to fix the price levels than is Government fiat. (News Conference, August 20, 1958).   [223

... **Policy.** The need of our times is for economic policies that, in the first place, recognize the proven sources of sustained economic growth and betterment, and in the second place, respect the need of people for a sense of security as well as opportunity in our complex, industrialized society. (Letter sent to Congress with Economic Report, January 20, 1955).   [224

EDUCATION

I believe that in the educational systems of the world today, in the faculties and in the student body, lie the good right arm of any commander's punch that is looking to knock out the enemy of international suspicion, selfish greed, and intolerance, which lead to war. (As Chief of Staff, upon

56

receiving Degree of Doctor of Laws at the University of Richmond, Va., March 28, 1946). [225

By promoting literacy and understanding, our schools have made it impossible for a specially privileged leisure class to prey on those who work. By opening the sciences and professions to all our people, our colleges and universities have destroyed the curse of inherited caste and made our society the most fluid yet attained by man. (As President of Columbia University, speech delivered to American Bar Association, St. Louis, Mo., September 5, 1949). [226

Education is one of those local functions that we should guard jealously because I found in every totalitarian state that I know anything about, one of the earliest efforts was to get charge of the educational processes. (As Republican Candidate for President, Abilene, Kansas, June, 1952). [227

The pursuit of truth, its preservation and wide dissemination; the achievement of freedom, its defense and propagation; these purposes are woven into the American concept of education. (Speech at Columbia University, New York, N. Y., May 31, 1954). [228

We believe that to take away the responsibility of communities and states in educating our children is to undermine not only a basic element of our freedom but a basic right of our citizens. (Message to Congress on Education, February 8, 1955). [229

Education is really bread and butter citizenship. It is just necessary to the developing of citizens that can do their, perform, their duties properly. (Press conference, Washington, D. C., February 9, 1955).   [230

If we believe Franklin and others who came after him, the educational process is absolutely necessary to the continuation of a vital democracy. There must be that understanding. (Speech at Washington Conference for the Advertising Council, April 2, 1957).   [231

...**College.**   Young people now in college must be equipped to live in the age of intercontinental ballistic missiles. However, what will then be needed is not just engineers and scientists, but a people who will keep their heads and, in every field, leaders who can meet intricate human problems with wisdom and courage. In short, we will need not only Einsteins and Steinmetzes, but Washingtons, and Emersons. (Speech at Municipal Auditorium, Oklahoma City, Okla., November 13, 1957).   [232

...**Cost.**   It is unwise to make education too cheap. If everything is provided freely, there is a tendency to put no value on anything. Education must always have a certain price on it; even as the very process of learning itself must always require individual effort and initiative. (Speech at Centennial Celebration Banquet of the National Education Association, Washington, D. C., April 4, 1957).   [233

...**Discipline.**   Education is a matter of discipline—and more, it is a matter of self-discipline. (Speech at Centennial Celebration Banquet of the National Education Association, Washington, D. C., April 4, 1957).   [234

... **Federal Aid.** Federal aid in a form that tends to lead to Federal control of our schools could cripple education for freedom. In no form can it ever approach the mighty effectiveness of an aroused people. But Federal leadership can stir America to national action. Then the nation's objective of the best possible education for all our young people will be achieved. (Message to Congress on Education, February 8, 1955). [235

... **Government Aid.** Our educational institutions should turn to government only for that which they themselves cannot accomplish at all or so well. (QUOTE, January 5, 1958, in letter to Dr. Kevin McCann, President of Defiance (Ohio) College). [236

... **Responsibility.** I deeply believe . . . that education is clearly a responsibility of state and local governments—and should remain so. (Speech over radio and television, Washington, D. C., May 14, 1957). [237

... **Scientific.** It takes time for a tree to grow, for an idea to become an accomplishment, for a student to become a scientist. Time is a big factor in two longer-term problems: strengthening our scientific education and our basic research. (Speech at Municipal Auditorium, Oklahoma City, Okla., November 13, 1957). [238

... **World.** I see no hope for the world except through education. (As Chief of Staff, address at dinner honoring President Daniel L. Marsh's Twentieth Anniversary at Boston University, Boston, Mass., January 31, 1946). [239

EMOTIONS

I think, when the heart is full, the tongue grows clumsy. (Speech to National Editorial Association, Washington, D. C., June 22, 1954). [240

EMPLOYMENT

The hardships of individuals and their families of a temporary downturn in employment are bad enough. But this administration is not going to be panicked by alarmists into activities that could actually make those hardships not temporary but chronic. (QUOTE, March 23, 1958, addressing Republican Women's National Conference, expressing opposition to "made work" projects). [241

ENGLAND

...America. The bond that joins us (England and U. S. A.)—stronger than blood lines, than common tongue and common law—is the fundamental conviction that man was created to be free, that he can be trusted with freedom, that governments have as a primary function the protection of his freedom. (As Supreme Allied Commander, Europe, speech delivered before the English Speaking Union, London, England, July 3, 1951). [242

...America. One hundred seventy-five years ago, the founding fathers of the American Republic declared their independence of the British Crown. Little could they have known—in the heat and bitterness of the hour—that the severance, accomplished in passion, would through the years flower into an alliance of such fitness and worth that it was never recorded on legal parchment, but in the hearts of our two peoples. (As Supreme Allied Commander, Europe, speech delivered before the English Speaking Union, London, England, July 3, 1951).   [243

EQUALITY

Equality is the basic concept of our whole Government—we must never forget it. (As Candidate for Republican nomination for President, speech at Detroit, Mich., June 14, 1952).   [244

Free government makes as its corner stone the concept, or the idea, that men are equal, they are equal before the law, they have equal rights and equal opportunities in the governments maintained to protect them. Now we know that men and women are not equal among themselves, physically— they are not equal among themselves mentally. Consequently, they must be equal if free government has any validity. They must be equal in some way that has nothing to do with the physical or intellectual make-up of man. And that can be only his spiritual side. (Speech to World Christian Endeavor Convention, Washington, D. C., July 25, 1954).   [245

We, a free people, cherishing equality for all, have never known, nor will we ever accept, any division of our nation into "little men" and "big men." We do not judge our neighbor or condemn him, by measuring the frontage of his property, the width of his television screen, or the wheel-base of his car. We believe—and we shall go on believing—that man was not created to bear such labels as "big" or "little." (Speech in Los Angeles, Calif., October 19, 1956).   [246

... **Justice.** We cannot claim the trust of hundreds of millions of people across Asia and Africa—if we, in a free America, do not ourselves hold high the banner of equality and justice for all. (Speech over radio and television, Washington, D. C., September 19, 1956).   [247

EUROPE

When I came back to Europe in January, 1951, after the ECA had been conceived and operating since its birth, I must tell you that the difference in spirit, the difference in the way people held up their heads; the difference in the pride which they were taking in their own nations, was little short of miraculous, in my mind. (As Allied Supreme Commander in Europe, views given to subcommittee of Senate Foreign Relations Committee in special hearing in Paris, France, July 9, 1951).   [248

While I think that most of us believe Europe has been doing about as much on the economic and financial side as its economy can stand, it does appear that there is room for action in a great field on moral and intellectual leadership. (News conference at Supreme Headquarters near Paris, France, January 22, 1952).   [249

... **East.** The captive people of Eastern Europe had made it evident that patriotism survives and that they continue to live in the hope of recovering their proud and honorable traditions of national independence. (Speech at North Atlantic Treaty Organization Council Meeting, Paris, France, December 16, 1957).   [250

... Marshall Plan. The effects of the Marshall Plan have been marked and have been important to the partial rehabilitation of Europe, but it would be false and idle to say that there does not exist in many strata of society pessimism bordering upon defeatism. (As General of the Army, speech to Members of Congress, Washington, D. C., February 1, 1951).   [251

... Unification. I am very hopeful that many of our problems would disappear if this whole area of Western Europe were one federal union. I believe it so strongly that I do not believe real security is going to be felt in the United States, in the British Empire, and other nations of the globe until that comes about. (As Allied Supreme Commander in Europe, views given to subcommittee of Senate Foreign Relations Committee in special hearing in Paris, France, July 9, 1951).   [252

... Unification. In my opinion, Europe must unite, far more closely (Western Europe, I am talking about) than it is now, or else there is no longterm settlement to all our difficulties. (Press conference, Paris, France, June 1952).   [253

... Unification. Our one trouble is that we are not united. It is a trouble the Communists don't have. They use a gun in the kidneys, a knife between the shoulder blades. People are united—or they don't exist. We have to find better ways. (QUOTE, June 1, 1952, addressing permanent council of NATO).   [254

... Western. Western Europe is so important to our future, our future is so definitely tied up with them, that we cannot afford to do less than our best in making sure that it does not go down the drain. (As General of the Army, speech to Members of Congress, February 1, 1951). [255

EXAMPLE

... America. We must realize that, as a nation, everything we say, everything we do, and everything we fail to say or do will have its impact in other lands. It will affect the minds and wills of men and women there. (As Republican Candidate for President, speech in San Francisco, Calif., October 8, 1952). [256

EXTREMISTS

... Patriotism. I don't think the U. S. needs superpatriots. We need patriotism, honestly practiced by all of us, and we don't need these people that are more patriotic than you or anybody else that's a man of good intent and tried to be a good citizen. That's just rot, if you'll excuse the word. (In television interview over CBS, November 23, 1961). [257

··F··

FACTS

...**Misleading.** Whoever misleads by calculated use of some but not all the facts, whoever distorts the truth to serve selfish ambition, whoever asserts weakness where strength exists—makes a mockery of the democratic process and misrepresents our beloved country in the eyes of the watching world. (Speech delivered at Republican National Convention, Chicago, Illinois, July 26, 1960).   [258

FAITH

The real fire within the builders of America was faith—faith in a Provident God whose hand supported and guided them; faith in themselves as the children of God . . . faith in their country and its principles that proclaimed man's right to freedom and justice. (Speech to homecoming gathering, Abilene, Kans., May 4, 1952).   [259

Faith was evidently too simple a thing for some to recognize in its paramount worth. Yet the present and the future demand men and women who are firm in their faith in our country and unswerving in their service to her. This is true in every basic unit of our political and social life—in the family, the community, the state and the nation. (Speech to Sixth National Assembly of the United Church Women, Atlantic City, N. J., October 6, 1953).   [260

Faith is the mightiest force that man has at his command. It impels human action to greatness in thought and word and in deed. (Speech to Assembly of the World Council of Churches, Evanston, Ill., August 19, 1954).   [261

FARMERS

I believe wholeheartedly and without any "ifs" or "buts" in Federal programs to stabilize farm prices, including the present program insuring 90 per cent of parity on all basic commodities. I believe that the farmers should obtain their full share of the national income. (As Republican Candidate for President, speech at Columbia, S. C., September 30, 1952).   [262

I am for ending this era in which, increasingly, the American farmers have been looked upon by the Department of Agriculture as Washington's stepchild. The independent American farmer is nobody's ward. And management and direction of the farm program—federally financed though it will be—must be turned over to farmers. It must be made, not only for them, but of and by them. (As Republican Candidate for President, speech at Columbia, S. C., September 30, 1952).   [263

Our farmers are the most efficient in the world. In no other country do so few people produce so much food to feed so many at such reasonable prices to consumers. (Speech over radio, Washington, D. C., April 16, 1956).   [264

FEAR

Fear is a climate that nourishes bankruptcy in dollars and morals alike. Those afraid seek security in a heedless extravagance that breeds waste of substance and corruption of men. Now if fear is long endured it wastes away material resources as well as our lives. In a climate of fear long endured, we can find the death rattle of a nation. (Address to American Legion Convention, New York, N. Y., August 25, 1952).   [265

We have not yet solved the problem of fear among the nations. The consequence is that not one government can exploit the resources of its own territory solely for the good of its people. (Address to Indian Parliament, New Delhi, India, December 10, 1959).   [266

FOOD

A hungry world is a restless and disturbed arena in which the agitator and political charlatan find ready followers, for men will sacrifice principle and peace to win food for their families. (As Chief of Staff, address at Veterans' Day, Nebraska State Fair, Lincoln, Nebr., September 1, 1946). [267

The twentieth century is unique in many ways—not the least of which is the fact that ours is the first generation which has dared to think in terms of food enough for all. (Address at Fifth International Congress on Nutrition, Washington, D. C., September 1, 1960).   [268

FOREIGN AFFAIRS

What we call foreign affairs is no longer foreign affairs. It's local affairs. Whatever happens in Indonesia is important to Indiana, whatever happens in any corner of the world has some effect on the farmer in Dickenson County, Kansas, or on a worker at a factory. (Speech at Graduation Ceremonies, Foreign Service Institute, June 12, 1959).   [269

FOREIGN AID

Mindful that world chaos is the enemy of our security, we have held out the hand of friendship to all, refraining from interference in the internal affairs of others. We have sought for all peoples the opportunity of choosing freely their form of government. Thereby we have accomplished much for humanity; had it not been for the policy of our government and the generosity of American men and women during the past two years, the world today would be in hopeless plight. (Speech to American Legion Convention, New York, N. Y., August 29, 1947).   [270

I do not believe that the U. S. can pick up the world on its economic, financial and material shoulders and carry it. We must have co-operation. (Speech in Library of Congress, February 1, 1951).   [271

We know that no nation may live by itself alone. To preserve the individual freedoms we prize so highly, we must not only protect ourselves as a nation, but we must make certain that others with like devotion to liberty may also survive and prosper. We have wanted a world in which we might live in peace and confidence, and in striving toward that goal we have understood that to help others was often the best way ourselves to advance. (Speech to Assembly of the World Council of Churches, Evanston, Ill., August 19, 1954). [272

We must use our skills and knowledge and, at times, our substance, to help others rise from misery, however far the scene of suffering may be from our shores. For wherever in the world a people knows desperate want, there must appear at least the spark of hope, the hope of progress—or there will surely rise at last the flames of conflict. (Second Inaugural Address, January 21, 1957). [273

No investment we make in our own security and peace can pay us greater dividends than necessary amounts of economic aid to friendly nations. (State of the Union Message, January 9, 1958). [274

Ever since its birth, the United States has gladly shared its wealth with others. This it has done without thought of conquest or economic domination. (Speech to General Assembly of the United Nations, New York, N. Y., August 13, 1958). [275

Of the amounts we devote to our own security and to peace, none yields a more beneficial return than the dollars we apply to the mutual efforts of the free world. (Speech over radio and television, Washington, D. C., December 3, 1959). [276

FOREIGN POLICY

The best foreign policy is to live our daily lives in honesty, decency and integrity; at home, making our own land a more fitting habitation for free men; and, abroad, joining with those of like mind and heart, to make all the world a place where all men can dwell in peace. (As President of Columbia University, 1st of a Series of Lectures Dedicated to the Cause of International Peace, Columbia University, New York, N. Y., April, 1950). [277

Our foreign policy must be clear, consistent and confident. This means that it must be the product of genuine, continuous cooperation between the executive and the legislative branches of this Government. It must be developed and directed in the spirit of true bipartisanship. (State of the Union Message, Washington, D. C., February 2, 1953). [278

We are trying to bring to men and women everywhere the right to go to sleep without fear that before morning, before next week, before next year, an atomic bomb will come screaming down out of the air to destroy them and their homes. (QUOTE, May 17, 1953). [279

Its (U. S. foreign policy's) guiding thought is this: we believe that we can permanently prosper and enjoy peace only as all peoples prosper and enjoy peace. (Speech on 15th Anniversary of the Voice of America, Washington, D. C., February 25, 1957). [280

FOREIGN RELATIONS

The mystery must be removed from foreign relations—our essential requirements and objectives must be clearly set forth for us all to read and to understand. Americans instinctively and properly dread the kind of secrecy that surrounded Yalta. (Speech to homecoming gathering, Abilene, Kans., May 4, 1952). [281

In our relations with all other nations, our attitude will reflect full recognition of their sovereign and equal status. We shall deal with common problems in a spirit of partnership. (Speech at 10th Anniversary Meeting of the United Nations, San Francisco, Calif., June 20, 1955). [282

FOREIGN TRADE

No one knows better than our enemies that our foreign trade is not just the frosting on our economic cake, but one of its essential ingredients. (As Republican Candidate for President, speech at Philadelphia, Pa., September 4, 1952). [283

Foreign trade means much more than the obtaining of vital raw materials from other nations. It means effectively strengthening our friends in the world at large—strengthening them not only to fortify their own economies—not only to be independent of direct financial aid from wealthier nations—but also to buy from us what we must sell to the world. (Speech at New Orleans, La., October 17, 1953). [284

We must recognize . . . that it is not possible for this nation, or any other nation, to produce enough of every metal and mineral needed by modern industry. These materials are not evenly distributed throughout the world. We have to depend on one another. (Message to Congress, March 30, 1954).   [285

FOREIGN TRAVEL

International travel has cultural and social importance in the free world. It also has economic significance. Foreign travel by Americans is a substantial source of dollars for many countries, enabling them to pay for what we sell them. (Message to Congress, March 30, 1954).   [286

FRANCE

We have been witnessing with sympathy and understanding the difficult days through which France has been passing . . . We look forward to a continuation of the intimate and friendly relations which have always characterized our long association with France. (QUOTE, June 8, 1958, welcoming Gen. Charles de Gaulle as Premier of France).   [287

FRANKNESS

Frankness, in good spirit, is a measure of friendship. (Speech to members of the Senate and Commons, House of Commons Chamber, Parliament Building, Ottawa, Canada, July 9, 1958).   [288

FREEDOM

Our nation is faced today with problems, present and future, which equal in scope and significance any it has hitherto met in 171 years of existence. Because we are close to them, it is difficult to recognize their historical import. But grave they are, almost beyond precedent, and they deal—as did our great crises of the past—with the freedom of man. What America does today, what America plans for tomorrow, can decide the sort of world the generations after us will possess—whether it shall be governed by justice or enslaved by force. (Address at American Legion Convention, New York, N. Y., August 29, 1947).   [289

Freedom, since the dawn of time, has been a hunger, God-set in the hearts of men. Always and everywhere, even though they may have never experienced it—even though they know its values only in their instincts rather than in their minds—men have sought personal liberty; have fought for it; have died for it. (Speech at Columbia University, New York, N. Y., May 31, 1954).   [290

In this day every resource of free men must be mustered if we are to remain free; every bit of our wit, our courage, and our dedication must be mobilized if we are to achieve genuine peace. There is no age nor group nor race that cannot somehow help. (Speech to Associated Press, New York, N. Y., April 25, 1955).   [291

We cannot doubt that the current of world history flows toward freedom. In the long run dictatorship and despotism must give way. We can take courage from that sure knowledge. (Speech to American Society of Newspaper Editors, Washington, D. C., April 21, 1956).   [292

The affairs of men do not stand still. The ideas of freedom will grow in vigor and influence—or they will gradually wither and die. If the area of freedom shrinks, the results for us will be tragic. Only if freedom continues to flourish will man realize the prosperity, the happiness, the enduring peace he seeks. (Speech to American Society of Newspaper Editors, Washington, D. C., April 21, 1956). [293

The struggle for human freedom has been a vital force in the history and progress of civilized mankind. In our highly interdependent modern society this struggle wherever waged, has necessarily become the common concern of all humanity. (Message to Hungary on their National Holiday, Washington, D. C., March 15, 1957). [294

We recognize that freedom is indivisible. Wherever in the world freedom is destroyed, by that much is every free nation hurt. (Speech over radio and television, Washington, D. C., March 16, 1959). [295

Our great strength is our dedication to freedom. And if we are sufficiently dedicated we will discipline ourselves so that we will make the sacrifices to do the thing that needs to be done. (Speech televised from London, England, August 31, 1959). [296

We must be concerned about threats to freedom, no matter where they may occur. (Speech over radio and television, Washington, D. C., September 10, 1959). [297

The struggle for freedom does not stop when the guns of war cease firing. Nor will it stop, so long as freedom is suppressed or threatened anywhere in the world. (Speech at dedication of Washington Memorial Building of the Veterans of Foreign Wars, Washington, D. C., February 8, 1960). [298

We all recognize that peace and fredom cannot be forever sustained by weapons alone. There must be a free world spirit and morale based upon the conviction that, for free men, life comprehends more than mere survival and bare security. Peoples everywhere must have opportunity to better themselves spiritually, intellectually, economically. (Speech over radio and television, Washington, D. C., February 21, 1960). [299

Freedom must be served as well as sought. It imposes duties and obligations, as well as bestowing rights and liberties. (Message to students of the Republic of Korea, August 2, 1960). [300

... **Individual.** Individual freedom is our most precious possession. It is to be guarded as the chief heritage of our people, the wellspring of our spiritual and material greatness, and the central target of all enemies—internal and external—who seek to weaken or destroy the American Republic. (As President of Columbia University, speech to American Bar Association, St. Louis, Mo., September 5, 1949). [301

... **Justice.** The destiny of man is freedom and justice under his Creator. Any ideology that denies this universal faith will ultimately perish or be recast. This is the first great truth that must underlie all our thinking, all our striving in this struggling world. (Speech at Baylor University, Waco, Tex., May 25, 1956).   [302

...**Knowledge.**   Wherever man's right to knowledge and the use thereof is restricted, man's freedom in the same measure disappears. (Speech to Columbia University Faculty Members, Alumni and Friends, New York, N. Y., May 31, 1954).   [303

...**Law.**   Freedom under law is like the air we breathe. People take it for granted and are unaware of it—until they are deprived of it. (Statement made for Law Day, April 30, 1958).   [304

...**Money.**   You could not keep any other country in the world free merely by money. You can't buy or import a heart, or a soul, or a determination to remain free. (Speech to National Editorial Association, Washington, D. C., June 22, 1954).   [305

...**Peace.**   Of all who inhabit the globe, only relatively small numbers—only a handful even in Russia itself—are fixed in their determination to dominate the world by force and fraud. Except for these groups in the several nations—mankind everywhere—those who still walk upright in freedom; those who must bow to communism; those who hesitate in neutralism—mankind everywhere hungers for freedom; well-being; peace. (Speech to Columbia University Faculty Members, Alumni and Friends, New York, N. Y., May 31, 1954).   [306

... **Self-Determination.** We do not believe that any nation, no matter how great, has a right to take another people and subject them to its rule. We believe that every nation has a right to live its own life. (Speech over radio and television, Washington, D. C., April 5, 1954). [307

... **Self-Determination.** Human beings everywhere, simply as an inalienable right of birth, should have freedom to choose their guiding philosophy, their form of government, their methods of progress. (Speech to Brazilian Congress, Rio de Janeiro, February 24, 1960). [308

... **Self-Discipline.** Freedom has been defined as the opportunity for self-discipline. This definition has a special application to the areas of wage and price policy in a free economy. Should we persistently fail to discipline ourselves, eventually there will be increasing pressure on Government to redress the failure. By that process freedom will step by step disappear. (State of the Union Message, Washington, D. C., January 10, 1957). [309

... **Speech.** Readiness to air a grievance, to propose a remedy, to argue the pros and cons of a plan, is an enduring—and priceless—American trait. (As President of Columbia University, speech to American Bar Association, St. Louis, Mo., September 5, 1949). [310

... **Speech.** Some of the most inspiring chapters in our history were written by a handful of our citizens who, joined together to talk out among themselves an idea or a principle, struck a note that revolutionized the world's thinking. That capacity still resides in every gathering in this country. (As President of Columbia University, speech to American Bar Association, St. Louis, Mo., September 5, 1949).   [311

... **Speech.**   Our system entitles every political voice to be heard—but let each voice be named and counted. Let every political medicine be offered in freedom's market place, but let it be plainly labeled—especially if it is poison. (Speech at Milwaukee, Wisc., October 3, 1952).   [312

... **Suppression.**   Whenever, and for whatever alleged reason, people attempt to crush ideas, to mask their convictions, to view every neighbor as a possible enemy, to seek some kind of divining rod by which to test for conformity, a free society is in danger. (Speech to Columbia University Faculty Members, Alumni and Friends, New York, N. Y., May 31, 1954).   [313

... **Truth.**   I do not believe without freedom you can be assured of the truth, and I do not believe that without truth you can long preserve freedom. (As President of Columbia University, speech to Associated Press, New York, N. Y., April 24, 1950).   [314

... **War.**   We know, and the world knows, that the American people will fight hostile and aggressive despotisms when their force is thrown against the barriers of freedom, when they seek to gain the high ground of power from which to destroy us. But we also know that to fight is the most costly way to keep America secure and free. Even an

America victorious in an atomic war could scarcely escape disastrous destruction of her cities and a fearful loss of life. Victory itself could be agony. (Speech over radio and television, Washington, D. C., May 21, 1957).   [315

FREE ENTERPRISE

When shallow critics denounce the profit motive inherent in our system of private enterprise, they ignore the fact that it is the economic support of every human right we possess and that without it all rights would soon disappear. (As President of Columbia University, Inaugural address, October 12, 1948).   [316

Our citizens have confidence in free enterprise as a means of achieving economic growth because we have seen it work. We know what it can do. (Speech to Tenth Colombo Plan Meeting, Seattle, Wash., November 10, 1958).   [317

FREE NATIONS

... Co-operation.   Co-operation among free nations is the key to common progress. Aid from one to another, if on a one-way-street basis, only and indefinitely continued, is not of itself truly productive. (Speech over radio and television, after tour of Latin America, Washington, D. C., March 8, 1960).   [318

FREE WORLD

I believe the free world has set for itself a certain goal. That goal is to achieve a military equilibrium in the areas in which we are concerned so that we can progress without fear, without hysteria, without particular hesitation toward the accomplishments of whatever our particular nations are trying to do in the way of the social benefits and gains of all their people. Because that's what governments are set up for. (Press conference in Paris, France, June, 1952).   [319

Even if we wanted to, we could not shut out the free world. We cannot escape its troubles. We cannot turn our backs on its hopes. We are an inseparable part of the free-world neighborhood. (Speech at dinner sponsored by the Committee for International Economic Growth and the Committee to Strengthen the Frontiers of Freedom, Washington, D. C., May 2, 1960).   [320

...**Communism.** The free nations of the world are under constant attack by international communism. This attack is planned on a broad front and carefully directed. Its ultimate goal is world domination. (News conference, Washington, D. C., July 2, 1958).   [321

...**Co-operation.** We must never allow ourselves to become so preoccupied with any differences between our two nations that we lose sight of the transcendent importance of free world co-operation in the winning of the global struggle. (Speech to members of the Senate and Commons, House of Commons Chamber, Parliament Building, Ottawa, Canada, July 9, 1958).   [322

...**Economy.** There must be a strong, free world economy so that free nations can support the military strength they need and also to help alleviate hunger, privation and despair, which the Communist leaders so successfully exploit. (Speech to American Legion Convention, Washington, D. C., August 30, 1954).   [323

... **Religion.**   The free world has one great factor in common. We are not held together by force, but we are held together by this great factor . . . The free world believes, under one religion or another, in a Divine Power, it believes in a Supreme Being. (Speech over radio and television, July 15, 1955).   [324

... **Russia.**   The issues that divide the free world from the Soviet bloc are grave and not subject to easy solution. But if good will exists on both sides, at least a beginning can be made. (Arriving in Paris, France, to attend Chiefs of State Meeting, May 15, 1960).   [325

FRIENDSHIP
Each of us, whether bearing a commission from his Government or traveling by himself for pleasure or for business, is a representative of the United States of America and he must try to portray America as he believes it in his heart to be: a peace-loving nation living in the fear of God but in the fear of God only, and trying to be partners with our friends. And we accept for a friend anyone who genuinely holds out the hand of friendship to us as we do to them. (Speech at New Orleans, La., October 17, 1953).   [326

The one mistake we must never make is to think of our friends in the international world as being tools of ours. They are not. They are friends of ours, and if they are not friends, they are uesless to us. (Speech over radio and tele-vision, Washington, D. C., April 5, 1954).   [327

For generations our country has been free from the devas-tation of war in her home land and is blessed with stanch and friendly neighbors. We covet no nation's possessions. We seek only the friendship of others. We are eager to repay this priceless gift in the same coin. (Speech to American Newspaper Publishers Association, New York, N. Y., April 22, 1954).   [328

This nation holds out the hand of friendship to all who would grasp it in sincerity . . . But we know that it is deeds and not words alone which count. (QUOTE, February 5, 1956, interview).   [329

We cherish our friendship with all nations that are or would be free. We respect, no less, their independence. And when, in time of want or peril, they ask our help, they may honorably receive it; for we no more seek to buy their sover-eignty than we would sell our own. Sovereignty is never bartered among free men. (Second Inaugural Address, Janu-ary 21, 1957).   [330

FUTURE
Let us always, even as we rightly revere the past and its heritage of freedom, never fear or doubt the future. For this—the future—is the hope and the home of all who are young and are free—if they are but brave. (Speech to National Young Republican Convention, Mt. Rushmore, S. Dak., June 11, 1953).   [331

Our future is in our own hands. Our prospects are limited only by our vision and our exertions. (Speech to Economic Mobilization Conference conducted by the American Management Association, New York City, N. Y., May 20, 1958). [332

As we peer into society's future, we—you and I, and our Government—must avoid the impulse to live only for today, plundering, for our own ease and convenience, the precious resources of tomorrow. (Speech over radio and television, Washington, D. C., January 17, 1961). [333

We cannot mortgage the material assets of our grandchildren without risking the loss also of their political and spiritual heritage. We want democracy to survive for all generations to come, not to become the insolvent phantom of tomorrow. (Speech over radio and television, Washington, D. C., January 17, 1961). [334

...**Past.** We cannot . . . face the future simply by walking into the past backwards. (As Presidential Nominee of the Republican Party, speech over radio and television, September 19, 1956). [335

...**Present.** Those who run too fast into the future sometimes trip over the present. (Speech at Republican Congressional testimonial dinner, Washington, D. C., June 1, 1961). [336

··G··

GERMANY

... **Berlin.** We have no intention of forfeiting our rights or of deserting a free people. Soviet rulers should remember that free men have, before this, died for so-called "scraps of paper" which represented duty and honor and freedom. (QUOTE, March 22, 1959, in radio and television broadcast). [337

... **Berlin.** Like our own Liberty Bell, Berlin's Freedom Bell is a tribute to those to whom freedom is more precious than life itself and a reminder that eternal vigilance is the price of liberty. (Letter to Willy Brandt, Mayor of W. Berlin, on Tenth Anniversary of Dedication of the Freedom Bell, October 20, 1960). [338

... **Berlin Wall.** There should have been an immediate denial of their right to do so (the building of the Berlin Wall by the Communists). In such matters as this, it becomes fact after a certain time. Therefore, the day the first stone or piece of wire was not pushed away by a tank defending the freedom of access . . . within hours it (the wall) became international fact. (Speech at Republican Party Forum, Los Angeles, Calif., April, 1964). [339

... **Germans.** The deliberate design of brutal world-wide rape that the German nation eagerly absorbed from the diseased brain of Hitler has met the fate for it by outraged justice. (V. E. Day broadcast, May 8, 1945). [340

... **Germans.** I believe in the freedom-loving quality of the German people . . . I would like to see the German people lined up with others in the defense of the Western type of civilization . . . Bygones are bygones. (Speech at Frankfurt, Germany, January 20, 1951). [341

... **Germans.** I have come to know there is a real difference between the regular German soldier and officer and Hitler and his criminal group . . . I do not believe that the German soldier, as such, has lost his honor. (QUOTE, January 28, 1951). [342

GOALS

... **America.** The goals for which America strives are not always easy of attainment. But we have an abiding determination to reach those goals without sacrifice of principle and to further the cause of freedom at home and abroad. (Speech recorded for broadcast to Americans overseas, July 4, 1959). [343

GOD

Without God there could be no American form of government, nor an American way of life. Recognition of the Supreme Being is the first—the most basic—expression of Americanism. Thus the founding fathers of America saw it, and thus, with God's help, it will continue to be. (QUOTE,

February 27, 1955, speech marking American Legion's "Back to God" movement). [344

... **And Man.** We are one nation, gifted by God with the reason and the will to govern ourselves, and returning our thanks to Him by respecting His supreme creation—the free individual. (Speech to Republican Party, Boston, Mass., September 21, 1953). [345

... **And Man.** We know that the Lord will give strength unto all of us as we strive tirelessly, confidently, for peace. (Speech at American Jewish Tercentenary Dinner, New York, N. Y., October 20, 1954). [346

... **And Man.** Oceans and great distances do not divide the human family in the sight of our Divine Creator. We are all His children. He teaches us to cherish and sustain one another. (Speech at Tenth Colombo Plan Meeting, Seattle, Wash., November 10, 1958). [347

... **And Man.** The core of our nation is belief in a Creator who has endowed all men with inalienable rights, including life, liberty and the pursuit of happiness. In that belief is our country's true hallmark, a faith that permeates every aspect of our political, social and family life. (Speech over radio and television, Washington, D. C., December 3, 1959). [348

GOVERNMENT

Our Government needs a searching going over by someone who has no obligation to the 20 years of building up that has been going on. We need a complete overhaul not only as to procedure and practice, but as to actual function and duty. (As Republican Candidate for President, news conference, Abilene, Kans., June 1952). [349

A Government that does not stir the pride of its own people cannot excite the respect of others. (As Republican Candidate for President, speech at Cincinnati, Ohio, September 22, 1952). [350

We need a Government that will arouse the pride of Americans as to win respect from other peoples. (As Republican Candidate for President, speech at Cincinnati, Ohio, September 22, 1952). [351

Government is nothing but individuals. Every one of the individuals in government belongs to you. He is your "boy" in some form or other. You put him there directly or indirectly. (Speech to 12th Annual Washington Conference of the Advertising Council, April 3, 1956). [352

Good government vitally concerns your business, your farm, your job, your home. It directly affects the prices you pay at the corner store. Good government is your own responsibility—not someone else's. (Speech in Los Angeles, Calif., October 20, 1958). [353

Constantly increasing acceptance of—and submission to—the influence of the federal government over so many phases of our lives and activities is the most serious threat to our American system. (QUOTE, December 16, 1962). [354

The best answer for too much Government in Washington is better government at home. (Speech to Life Insurance Association of America, New York City, N. Y., December 9, 1964).   [355

Too much government planes off peaks of excellence, hones down differences, dries up competition and leaves a drab and unhappy community where once dwelt thrift, zeal to excel and ambition for human betterment. (Speech to Life Insurance Association of America, New York City, N. Y., December 9, 1964).   [356

An overpowerful government can rob a whole people, just as surely as a pickpocket can steal from an individual. (Speech to Life Insurance Association of America, New York City, N. Y., December 9, 1964).   [357

... **Administration.**   The first step toward winning a peace that we can trust to endure is to establish in Washington an administration which we ourselves can trust. We will win this battle for peace only after we have won the Battle of Washington. (As Republican Candidate for President, speech in Philadelphia, Pa., September 4, 1952).   [358

... **Administration: Policies.**   What Washington is in need of is not new administrators of the policies of the old Administration; but a new administration with new policies. (As Republican Candidate for President, speech in Philadelphia, Pa., September 4, 1952).   [359

... **Aid.**   I personally still adhere to Lincoln's generalization. You must do for people what they cannot do for them-

88

selves or so well do in their individual capacities, but, in other things government ought not to interfere. (Press conference, January 30, 1957).   [360

...Aid.   At the very least might we not defer buying tickets for a trip to the moon until we can pay cash for the ride; and do so without mortgaging the old homestead to repair a leaky roof? Addiction to a soft-headed philosophy that federal money can cure every national ill could undermine one of the greatest resources of America—the sturdiness of and self-dependence of the individual citizen; it could ultimately cost our people their liberty. (Speech in Chicago, Ill., September 16, 1961).   [361

...Bureaucracy.   Bureaucracy—helpless to lead older nations to security and prosperity—will do no better in America . . . The Federal Government must be so organized that we feel confident we haven't lost sight of such things as thrift, frugality, economy. (Speech to homecoming gathering, Abilene, Kans., May 4, 1952).   [362

...Bureaucracy.   There is—in our affairs at home—a middle way between untrammelled freedom of the individual and the demands for the welfare of the whole nation. Thus we must avoid government by bureaucracy as carefully as it avoids neglect of the helpless. (State of the Union Message, Washington, D. C., February 2, 1953).   [363

...Centralization.   No central group can sustain the strength of a free economy, and the liberty guaranteed by our founding fathers. (QUOTE, June 10, 1962).   [364

... Conduct. A word about conduct in government: Here there is only one principle for all Americans to follow; the standard of official conduct must be the highest standard known to human behavior. (Speech to Republican Women's National Conference, Washington, D. C., March 18, 1958).   [365

... Controls. I believe that if you have to resort, in time of peace, to strict governmental control of prices, of wages, services and things, then we are abandoning the system that has made us great and by which we have lived and in which we believe. (News conference, June 26, 1957).   [366

... Controls. The unending drive for federal domination of the nation's power and water resources, and the ever-increasing federal involvement in urban problems, agriculture, housing, care of the youth and the aged, the ill and the poor, and the temporarily unemployed, can only end—if unchecked—in a dangerous centralization of power. Continued, this tendency will ultimately destroy the will and the ability of the individual and community to govern themselves. (Speech in Chicago, Ill., September 16, 1961).   [367

... Cost. Every real American is proud to carry his share of any burden. In war and peace, I have seen countless examples of American pride and of the unassuming but inspiring courage of young American citizens. I simply do not believe for one second that anyone privileged to live in this country wants someone else to pay his own fair and just share of the cost of his government. (Speech over radio and television, Washington, D. C., March 15, 1954).   [368

...Decisions. One of my predecessors is said to have observed that in making his decisions he had to operate like a football quarterback—he could not very well call the next play until he saw how the last play turned out. Well, that may be a good way to run a football team, but in these times it is no way to run a government. (Speech to Republican National Convention, San Francisco, Calif., August 23, 1956).   [369

...Defense. The American people need a government that knows enough about arms and armies to work out the most defense at less cost with the least delay. (As Republican Candidate for President, speech at Cincinnati, Ohio, September 22, 1952).   [370

. . . Despotism. With the passage of time, despotic government historically has suffered internal decay before it is apparent on the surface. (Speech to North Atlantic Treaty Organization Council Meeting, Paris, France, December 16, 1957).   [371

...Economy. If solvency and security are not synonymous, they are so closely related that the difference, if any, is scarcely discernible. (Speech to Carnegie Institute, Pittsburgh, Pa., October 19, 1950).   [372

...Economy. Government—while it cannot guarantee prosperity—has a continuing responsibility in times like these to use its powers to help counteract recession. It has a duty to alleviate human hardship and protect our human resources, to help promote an upturn in production and employment, and to help build a solid foundation for longterm growth. All this it should seek to do in a way that strengthens the vitality of our private enterprise system, and that includes safeguarding the integrity of our currency. (Speech to Economic Mobilization Conference Conducted by the American Management Association, New York City, N. Y., May 20, 1958).   [373

... **Employees.**   The safety of America and the trust of the people alike demand that the personnel of the Federal Government be loyal in their motives and reliable in the discharge of their duties. Only a combination of both loyalty and reliability promises genuine security. (State of the Union Message, Washington, D. C., February 2, 1953).
                                                                                    [374

... **Employees.**   The vast bulk of your federal employees comprise dedicated and able citizens. I respect and honor them. (Speech to National Young Republican Convention, Mt. Rushmore, S. Dak., June 11, 1953).   [375

... **Hydroelectric Power.**   It is not properly a Federal responsibility to try to supply all the power needs of our people. The Federal Government should no more attempt to do so than it should assume responsibility for supplying all their drinking water, their food, their housing and their transportation. (Speech at dedication of McNary Dam, Ore., September 23, 1954).   [376

... **Individuals.**   The aspirations of most of our people can best be fulfilled through their own enterprise and initiative, without government interference. This Administration, therefore, follows two simple rules: first, the Federal Government should perform an essential task in this field only when it cannot otherwise be adequately performed; and second, in performing that task, our Government must not impair the self-respect, the freedom and the incentive of the individual. So long as these two rules are observed, the Government can and must fully meet its obligations without creating a dependent population or a domineering bureaucracy. (State of the Union Message, January 6, 1955).   [377

... **Labor.** If the government charges impatiently into every major (labor) dispute, the negotiations between parties will become a pointless preliminary farce, while everyone waits around to see what the government will do. (Speech to Republican National Convention, San Francisco, Calif., August 23, 1956).   [378

... **Laws.** Free men . . . agree upon certain rules—which we call laws—and maintain political agents, or governments, to codify and enforce upon us all these self-imposed rules. In free countries, the agent may never become the master; if human rights and freedoms are to flourish, government must operate with its powers sharply defined and limited *by* the governed. And unless we understand this, the American Dream may become the American Nightmare. (As President of Columbia University, speech to New York Herald Tribune Forum, New York, N. Y., October 25, 1949).   [379

... **Local.** Dishonesty in a city council is as evil as in a Federal bureau. If corruption is eliminated in these local

93

offices where we have intimate knowledge of each candidate, it will disappear in the higher places of government. (Speech to homecoming gathering, Abilene, Kans., May 4, 1952). [380

... **Local.** I believe that the greatest amount of authority, which means comparable responsibility, must be retained in the localities in our country or we are working steadily away from the system of government that has made this country great, because that kind of system exploits private initiative, local initiative, local care for the expenditures. (Press conference, Washington, D. C., February 9, 1955). [381

... **Loyalty Tests.** To work for the U. S. Government is a privilege, not a right. And it is the prerogative of the government to set the strictest test upon the loyalty and the patriotism of those entrusted with our nation's safety. (As Republican Candidate for President, speech in Milwaukee, Wis., October 3, 1952). [382

... **Obligations.** The legislative program that you and I support is . . . designed to protect our freedoms, to foster a growing, prosperous peacetime economy, and to fulfill the Government's obligations in helping solve the human problems of our citizenry. (Speech to 500 district leaders of the National Citizens for Eisenhower Congressional Committee, Washington, D. C., June, 1954). [383

... **Officials.** When I speak of brains and will power, I am speaking of the two most essential, utterly indispensable needs of our government in the winning of the peace. Either, without the other, will fail. It is not hard to find men long on courage and short on brains. But this is no time for boldness without reflection and purpose. (As Republican Candidate for President, speech in Cincinnati, Ohio, September 22, 1952).   [384

... **Paternalistic.** All agree it is criminal for one man to steal from another. But over-powerful government can rob the individual just as surely—only the scale is grander, the stakes are greater, and the loss far more tragic. For what is stolen by paternalistic government is that precious compound of initiative, independence and self-respect that distinguishes a man from the mob, a person from a number, a free man from the slave. (Address at Republican fundraising dinner, Washington, D. C., June 1, 1961).   [385

... **Philosophy.** There is—in world affairs—a steady course to be followed between an assertion of strength that is truculent and a confession of helplessness that is cowardly. There is—in our affairs at home—a middle way between untrammeled freedom of the individual and the demands for the welfare of the whole nation. (QUOTE, February 8, 1953).   [386

... **Regulation.** Those who want the government to regulate matters of the mind and spirit are like men who are so afraid of being murdered that they commit suicide to avoid assassination. (Speech at National Archives, Washington, D. C., at dedication of new shrine for the Declaration of

Independence, the Constitution and the Bill of Rights, December 15, 1952).   [387

... **Self.** Internally and externally any form of government, and particularly self-government, is always subject to some kind of attack, particularly successful government that has brought material prosperity in the measure which ours has. (Speech to 12th Annual Washington Conference of the Advertising Council, April 3, 1956).   [388

... **Self-Discipline.** I believe that responsibility of self-discipline, balance, common sense and faith in the individual and locality are indispensable to the perpetuation and functioning of self-government. (Speech at Testimonial Dinner for Sen. Everett Dirksen, Chicago, Ill., September 16, 1961).   [389

... **Spending.** I believe deeply that continuing deficit spending is immoral. It forces our children to support spendthrift parents. It visits upon voteless youngsters a mountain of unpaid bills. It is government by credit card, with the bill to be paid by our children not merely in money but also in liberty. (Speech at Republican Congressional Testimonial Dinner, Washington, D. C., June 1, 1961).
[390

... **Spending.** Our material strength rests on a free, competitive enterprise, generating a steadily expanding economy measured always in a stable and respected currency, worth next month, next year, next decade what it is worth tonight. That is why I have in these times so gravely viewed unnecessary federal spending. It weakens power and confidence abroad. (Speech in Chicago, Ill., September 16, 1961). [391

... **States.** Unless we preserve in this country the place of the state government, its traditional place, with the power, the authority, the responsibilities and the revenues necessary to discharge those responsibilities, then we are not going to have America as we have known it; we will have some other form of government. (Speech to forty-fifth Annual Governors' Conference, Seattle, Wash., August 4, 1953).   [392

... **Subversion.** No one could be more determined than I that any kind of communistic subversive or pinkish influence be uprooted from responsible places in our government. Make no mistake about it. (As Republican Candidate for President, questioned by news reporters, Abilene, Kans., June 1952).   [393

... **Subversion.** There are those who believe that any means are justified by the end of rooting out Communism. There are those who believe that the preservation of democracy and the preservation of the soul of freedom in this country can and must be accomplished with decency and fairness and due process of law. I belong to this second school. But at the same time, I say to you that no differences in theory can excuse any failure to see that Communist contamination inside our government is stamped out. (Speech in Chicago, Ill., October 31, 1952).   [394

... **Support.** Whatever, in time of real crisis, the government directs, each of us must give his support, because we're going to have to talk with one voice if anything critical does happen. (Interview, on situation in Cuba, January, 1963).   [395

... **Talent.** We need intelligent, creative, steady political leadership as at no time before in our history. There must be more talent in government—the best our nation affords. (QUOTE, June 12, 1960, commencement address at Notre Dame University, South Bend, Ind.). [396

... **Trust.** The American people want a government which merits their trust because, from top to bottom, it is trustworthy. (As Republican Candidate for President, speech at Columbia, S. C., September 30, 1952). [397

GROWTH

... **Stability.** We must have growth that does not endanger stability; we must have stability that does not throttle growth. (Speech to Boards of Governors of the International Bank for Reconstruction and Development, the International Monetary Fund and the International Finance Corporation, Washington, D. C., September 23, 1957). [398

··H··

HEALTH

Rarely have I known any time in my life when I had to be concerned about my own physical feeling, outside of a flu or a cold or something like that. I have been one of those fortunate creatures in good health. Now, at times, unquestionably, I feel more tired than, I think, I would have in the past, but that may be also just advancing years. (In press and radio conference, Washington, D. C., February 8, 1956).   [399

Some of my medical advisers believe that adverse effects on my health will be less in the Presidency than in any other position I might hold. They believe that because of the watchful care that doctors can and do exercise over a President, he normally runs less risk of physical difficulty than do other citizens. (Speech over radio and television, Washington, D. C., February 29, 1956).   [400

HEALTH INSURANCE

Federal compulsion, with our health supervised under a Washington stethoscope, is not American and it is not the answer . . . It would give us poorer medical care. The answer is to build on the system of voluntary nonprofit health-insurance plans . . . The usefulness of federal loans or other aid to local health plans should be explored. (As Republican Candidate for President, remarks on health insurance, October 1952). [401

HIGHWAYS

The country urgently needs a modernized inter-state highway system to relieve existing congestion, to provide for the expected growth of motor vehicle traffic, to strengthen the Nation's defenses, to reduce the toll of human life exacted each year in highway accidents, and to promote economic development. (Letter sent to Congress with economic report, January 24, 1956). [402

HISTORY

Occasional pages of history do record the faces of the "Great Destroyers" but the whole book of history reveals mankind's never-ending quest for peace and mankind's God-given capacity to build. (Speech to General Assembly of United Nations, December 8, 1953). [403

HOPE

No military victory, no diplomatic triumph, no precision-perfect foreign policy of our own can mean very much for very long—if it does not bring hope to hundreds of millions of people who live today in fear or need or hunger. As surely as we seek lasting peace, we shall find it only as these people come to have faith in their own future in freedom. (Speech over radio, Washington, D. C., August 6, 1953). [404

The world's hope . . . depends upon the strength of our national life; the force of our leadership, the integrity of our government, the daily well-being of our people, the vigor of our economy, the might of our resources. (Speech over radio and television, Portland, Ore., October 18, 1956).   [405

. . . Despair.   Hope spurs humans everywhere to work harder, to endure more now that the future may be better; but despair is the climate of war and death. (As President of Columbia University, First of a Series of Lectures Dedicated to the Cause of International Peace, Columbia University, New York, N. Y., April, 1950).   [406

HOPEFULNESS

We cannot afford to be negligent or complacent, but we must be hopeful. (Speech over radio and television, Washington, D. C., July 25, 1955).   [407

HOPELESSNESS

Hopelessness makes men prey to any promise of better existence, even the most false and spurious. (Speech to American Society of Newspaper Editors, Washington, D. C., April 21, 1956).   [408

HUMAN BEINGS

. . . Enrichment.   We must . . . seek with new vigor, new initiative, the path to a peace based on the effective control of armaments, on economic advancement and on the freedom of all peoples to be ruled by governments of their choice. Only thus can we exercise the full capacity God has given us to enrich the lives of the individual human beings who are our ultimate concern, our responsibility and our strength. (Speech to General Assembly of United Nations, New York, N. Y., August 13, 1958). [409

HUMAN RIGHTS

When our forefathers prepared the immortal document that proclaimed our independence, they asserted that every individual is endowed by his Creator with certain inalienable rights. As we gaze back through history to that date, it is clear that our Nation has striven to live up to this declaration, applying it to nations as well as to individuals. (State of the Union Message, Washington, D. C., January 10, 1957). [410

HUMILITY

Humility must always be the portion of any man who receives acclaim earned in the blood of his followers and the sacrifices of his friends. (Speech at the Guildhall, London, England, June 12, 1945). [411

HUMOR

We must keep our sense of humor always—for, since time immemorial man has heard no cry more agonized than that of the deposed bureaucrat or the demoted politician. (Speech to National Young Republican Convention, Mt. Rushmore, S. Dak., June 11, 1953). [412

HUMPHREY, GEORGE M.

A friendship of the strength and depth of ours cannot suffer merely because of your departure from Washington. (Letter to George M. Humphrey, Secretary of the Treasury, on his retirement, May 29, 1957). [413

HUNGARY

The terror imposed upon Hungary (by Soviet officials) repudiates and negates every article in the Declaration of Human Rights. (QUOTE, December 16, 1956, speech marking Human Rights Day). [414

HUNGER

As long as the majority of human beings have to go through a brutish daily struggle for enough to eat it is foolish to talk of world peace. (QUOTE, June 4, 1950, as President of Columbia University). [415

In vast stretches of the earth, men awoke today in hunger. They will spend the day in unceasing toil. And as the sun goes they will still know hunger. They will see suffering in the eyes of their children . . . So long as this is so, peace and freedom will be in danger throughout our world. For whenever free men lose hope of progress, liberty will be weakened and the seeds of conflict will be sown. (Speech to Tenth Colombo Plan Meeting, Seattle, Wash., November 10, 1958). [416

Today we have the scientific capacity to abolish from the world at least this one evil; we can eliminate the hunger that emaciates the bodies of children, that scars the souls of their parents, that stirs the passions of those who toil endlessly and earn only scraps. (Remarks at Agriculture Fair, New Delhi, India, December 11, 1959). [417

. . . **Malnutrition.** For the first time in history the world is nearing victory over man's ancient enemies—hunger and malnutrition. They are not whipped but ours is the first generation to catch the scent. (QUOTE, September 11, 1960, speech to International Congress on Nutrition, Washington, D. C.). [418

... **Peace.** Peace will be without real meaning—it may even be unattainable—until the peoples of the world have finally overcome the natural enemies of humanity—hunger, privation and disease. (Speech to Iranian Parliament, Tehran, December 14, 1959). [419

... **War.** Prosperous nations are not war hungry, but a hungry nation will always seek war if it has to in desperation. (Speech at dinner in his honor by City of New York, June 19, 1945). [420

HYDROGEN BOMB

What will it profit us to achieve the H-bomb and survive that tragedy or triumph, if the generations that succeed us must starve in a world, because of our misuse, grown barren as the mountains of the moon? (As President of Columbia University, First of a Series of Lectures dedicated to the Cause of International Peace, Columbia University, New York, N. Y., April, 1950). [421

·· I ··

IDEAS

... **Good.** The world moves, and ideas that were good once are not always good. (Press conference, Washington, D. C., August 31, 1955).   [422

IMMIGRANTS

It is a manifest right of our Government to limit the number of immigrants our nation can absorb. It is also a manifest right of our Government to set reasonable requirements on the character and the numbers of the people who come to share our land and our freedom. It is well for us, however, to remind ourselves occasionally of an equally manifest fact; we are—one and all—immigrants or sons and daughters of immigrants. (State of the Union Message, Washington, D. C., February 2, 1953).   [423

IMMIGRATION

It is imperative that our immigration policy be in the finest American tradition of providing a haven for oppressed peoples and fully in accord with our obligation as a leader of the free world. (State of the Union Message, Washington, D. C., January 12, 1961).   [424

... Hungarian Refugees. I think that it is particularly regrettable that the Congress did not provide a method whereby the thousands of brave and worthy Hungarian refugees, who have suffered so much at the hands of communism, might in the future acquire permanent residence looking forward to citizenship. (Statement made after Amendment to Immigration Act became Law, September 11, 1957). [425

IMPOSSIBILITIES

When you finally find something that must be done, impossibilities disappear and become merely major obstacles. (As Supreme Commander of Allied Forces in Europe, press conference, Paris, France, January 12, 1952). [426

INDIVIDUAL EFFORT

The constant danger to democracy lies in the tendency of the individual to hide himself in the crowd—to defend his own failure to act forthrightly according to conviction under the false excuse that the effort of one in one hundred forty million has no significance. (As Chief of Staff, speech at Norwich University, Northfield, Vt., June 9, 1946). [427

No matter how much wisdom may go into planning, whether it be an insurance program, an armed invasion of a continent, a campaign to reduce the inroads of disease, the measure of its success always will be spirit and mettle of the individuals engaged in its execution. (As Chief of Staff, speech to National Board of Fire Underwriters, New York, N. Y., May 27, 1947). [428

INDIVIDUALITY

More than ever before, in our country, this is the age of the individual. Endowed with the accumulated knowledge of centuries, armed with all the instruments of modern science, he is still assured personal freedom and wide avenues of expression so that he may win for himself, his family and his country greater material comfort, ease and happiness; greater spiritual satisfaction and contentment. (As President of Columbia University, speech at Commencement Exercises, Columbia University, New York, N. Y., June 1, 1949). [429

A fundamental belief shines forth in this Republic. We believe in the worth and dignity of the individual. We know that if we are to govern ourselves wisely—in the tradition of America—we must have the opportunity to develop our individual capacities to the utmost. (State of the Union Message, Washington, D. C., January 5, 1956). [430

INDIVIDUALS

... Dignity. The supreme belief of our society is in the dignity and freedom of the individual. To the respect of that dignity, to the defense of that freedom, all effort is pledged. (Speech to Republican Party, Boston, Mass., September 21, 1953). [431

INEVITABILITY

It has always been my faith that eventual triumph of decency and freedom and right in this world is inevitable. But, as a wise American once observed, it takes a lot of hard work and sacrifice by a lot of people to bring about the inevitable. (Speech at Municipal Auditorium, Oklahoma City, Okla., November 13, 1957). [432

INFERIORITY COMPLEX

I think some young people feel they have to demonstrate, wear their hair long and call attention to themselves because they are suffering from an inferiority complex. They have to make themselves seen and heard in some way. They are gaining headlines—but they are creating an image of American youth that is false. (Interview, Gettysburg, Pa., November, 1966). [433

INFLATION

At its worst, inflation can insidiously destroy the fruits of a whole lifetime's labor. Even at a gradual pace, inflation dooms the farmer and city dweller alike to a hopeless treadmill race against the cost of living. (Speech to homecoming gathering, Abilene, Kans., May 4, 1952). [434

In our kind of economy, inflation, unless brought under control, eventually leads to depression. Inflation can even destroy free, competitive enterprise—the indispensable economic support to human liberty. (Speech to homecoming gathering, Abilene, Kans., May 4, 1952). [435

Prolonged inflation could be as destructive of a truly free economy as could a chemical attack against an army in the field. (Speech over radio, Washington, D. C., May 19, 1953). [436

Our own history shows that those who most severely suffer from inflation are not great banks or colossal corporations—but all our citizens, especially our older people who depend upon fixed incomes, life insurance, pensions or Social Security payments. (As Republican Nominee for President, speech in Los Angeles, Calif., October 19, 1956). [437

Among the basic problems on your agenda none is currently more pressing than inflation—the tendency to rising prices. While this tendency is stronger at some times than others, and in some places more than others, it is a worldwide phenomenon today. (Speech to Boards of Governors of the International Bank for Reconstruction and Development, the International Monetary Fund and the International Finance Corporation, Washington, D. C., September 23, 1957). [438

If our efficiency in production and the payments which we make for productive efforts of all sorts rise in step in coordination, there is no impetus to rising prices. But if our efficiency does not increase, if our productivity does not rise, we as nations will end to fall into the costly error of overpaying ourselves for the work we do. Along that road . . . lies the spur to further inflation. (Speech to the Boards of Governors of the International Bank for Reconstruction and Development, the International Monetary Fund and the International Finance Corporation, Washington, D. C., September 23, 1957). [439

We must fight inflation as we would a fire that imperils our home. Only by so doing can we prevent it from destroying our salaries, savings, pensions, and insurance, and from gnawing away the very roots of a free, healthy economy and the Nation's security. (State of the Union Message, Washington, D. C., January 7, 1960). [440

Inflation is bad. It is bad whether generated by spendthrift government or by industrial price abuses. It is no less bad if caused by unjustified wage increases, or by demands of self-preserving pressure groups. One of its sources is a lack of a sense of responsibility. (Speech at Testimonial Dinner for Sen. Everett Dirksen, Chicago, Ill., September 16, 1961). [441

INFORMATION SERVICE

I believe that the U. S. needs a very, very much stronger information service. In our case I would not call it propaganda, because the truth is all we need. We do not have to falsify the record nor our intentions. (As General of the Army, speech to Members of Congress, Washington, D. C., February 1, 1951). [442

INTEGRATION

... Little Rock, Ark. When I became President, I took an oath to support and defend the Constitution of the United States. The only assurance I can give you is that the Federal Constitution will be upheld by me by every legal means at my command. (Telegram to Gov. Faubus of Ark., September 5, 1957). [443

... Little Rock, Ark. I recognize the inescapable responsibility resting upon the Gov. (Faubus) to preserve law and order in his state. I am gratified by his constructive and cooperative attitude at our meeting. I have assured the Governor of the cooperation of Federal officials. (Statement issued September 14, 1957). [444

... **Little Rock, Ark.** I am confident that the citizens of the city of Little Rock and the State of Arkansas will welcome this opportunity to demonstrate that in their city and in their state proper orders of the U. S. Constitution will be executed promptly and without disorder. (Statement issued September 21, 1957). [445

... **Little Rock, Ark.** It will be a sad day in this country—both at home and abroad—if school children can safely attend their classes only under the protection of armed guards. (Statement issued September 23, 1957). [446

... **Little Rock, Ark.** Mob rule cannot be allowed to override the decisions of the courts. (Speech over radio and television, September 24, 1957). [447

INTELLIGENCE

In the work of intelligence, heroes are undecorated and unsung, often even among their own fraternity. Their inspiration is rooted in patriotism; their reward can be little except the conviction that they are performing a unique and indispensible service for their country and the knowledge that America needs and appreciates their efforts. (Remarks at cornerstone laying ceremonies for Central Intelligence Agency Building, Langley, Va., November 3, 1959). [448

INTERNATIONAL GEOPHYSICAL YEAR

As I see it . . . the most important result of the International Geophysical Year is that demonstration of the ability of peoples of all nations to work together harmoniously for the common good. I hope this can become common practice in other fields of human endeavor. (Remarks over radio and television, June 30, 1957).   [449

INTOLERANCE

The final battle against intolerance is to be fought—not in the chambers of any legislature—but in the hearts of men. (As Republican Nominee for President, speech in Los Angeles, Calif., October 19, 1956).   [450

ISOLATIONISM

No nation's security and well-being can be lastingly achieved in isolation, but only in effective cooperation with fellow-nations. (Speech to American Society of Newspaper Editors, Washington, D. C., April 16, 1953).   [451

It seems quite clear that free government could not possibly exist in any one nation alone. If any country, no matter how powerful, were an island of representative or free or democratic government, surrounded by dictators, it would soon wither away and die. It would, itself, have to become a dictatorship. (Speech to 42nd Conference of the Interparliamentary Union, Washington, D. C., October 9, 1953). [452

Nowhere on this planet today is there an impregnable fortress, a continent or island so distant that it can ignore all the outer world. (Speech to American Newspaper Publishers Association, New York, N. Y., April 22, 1954).   [453

No people can live to itself alone. The unity of all who dwell in freedom is their only sure defense. The economic need of all nations—is mutual dependence—makes isolation an impossibility; not even America's prosperity could long survive if other nations did not prosper. No nation can long be a fortress, lone and strong and safe. And any people, seeking such shelter for themselves, can now build only their own prison. (Second Inaugural Address, January 21, 1957).   [454

· · J · ·

JUDGMENT

Good judgment seeks balance and progress; lack of it eventually finds imbalance and frustration. (Speech over radio and television, Washington, D. C., January 17, 1961).   [455

...Honor. The right to question or challenge a man's judgment carries with it no automatic right to question his honor. (Speech in Milwaukee, Wisc., October 3, 1952).   [456

JUSTICE

The steady purpose of our society is to assure justice, before God, for every individual. We must be ever alert that freedom does not wither through the careless amassing of restrictive controls or the lack of courage to deal boldly with the giant issues of the day. (State of the Union Message, Washington, D. C., January 7, 1960).   [457

...Freedom. In the light of our world position, our nation cannot tolerate, in any individual or in any party, demogoguery that would put winning a cheap political advantage above winning the world struggle for justice and freedom. (Speech to Republican Women's National Conference, Washington, D. C., March 18, 1958).   [458

·· K ··

KNOWLEDGE
Knowledge is or should be universal; it was meant to be shared; and it has the peculiar quality about it that, when its parts are brought together, the result is a multiplication rather than a mere addition of those values. (Speech to Foreign Educators participating in the International Teacher Development Program, Washington, D. C., September 16, 1959). [459

... Use. No matter how much intellectual luggage we carry around in our heads, it becomes valuable only if we know how to use the information—only if we are able to relate one fact of a problem to the others do we truly understand them. (Speech at Gettysburg College, Pa., April 4, 1959). [460

KOREA
The South Koreans' only crime has been the desire to live their own lives as they choose, at peace with the rest of the world. The American decision to assist them was inescapable. The alternative would be another kind of Munich. (Speech at Valley Forge, July 4, 1950). [461

There is no sense in the United Nations, with America bearing the brunt . . . being constantly compelled to man those front lines (in Korea). That is a job for the Koreans. We do not want Asia to feel that the white man of the West is his enemy. If there must be a war there, let it be Asians against Asians, with our support on the side of freedom. (As Republican Candidate for President, October, 1952). [462

There are many limitations in a war of this kind, but this much is certain: Here we are realizing that freedom is an indivisible thing—we're all engaged in a common enterprise and that common enterprise, even if we have not been able to state its objectives in definite, concrete terms, and if there may be some misunderstandings or differences of opinion with respect to that—still we are all here to see it through. (Press conference after trip to Korean front, December, 1952). [463

I let it be known that if there were not going to be an armistice that I would no longer regard this war as being limited to deny ourselves the right to attack wherever we saw enemy coming at us—meaning that we were not going to be bound by the kind of weapons we would use. (In a national educational television network interview broadcast, September 18, 1966). [464

I don't mean to say that we'd have used those great big things (nuclear weapons) and destroyed cities, but we would use them enough to win and we, of course, would have tried to keep them on military targets, not civil targets. (In a national educational television network interview broadcast, September 18, 1966). [465

· · L · ·

LABOR

I have no use for those—regardless of their political party
—who hold some foolish dream of spinning the clock back
to days when unorganized labor was a huddled, almost helpless mass. (As Republican Candidate for President, speech to
American Federation of Labor, New York, N. Y., September
17, 1952).   [466

The history of labor is studded with the names of men
and women who have inspired our working people, our
country and mankind. In their example you can at home
help toward a better citizenship and nation. Abroad you can
help liberate hundreds of millions from misery and slavery.
(QUOTE, December 11, 1955, telephone message to dele-
gates of newly-merged AFL-CIO Unions).   [467

... Communism.   I should like to commend the American Federation of Labor. Your history of absolute opposition
to communism in all its forms, in whatever way it may pose
its threat, is to me a heartening thing, and at least in that we
are one, and I am certain there is no difference possible
between us. (Speech to annual convention of American

Federation of Labor, Los Angeles, Calif., September 24, 1954).   [468

...**Communism.** I also recommend and stated that I would recommend measures for making certain that people in organized labor were not compelled to take an oath they were anti-Communist, particularly when no one else had to do so. I think that is completely un-American. (Speech to annual convention of American Federation of Labor, Los Angeles, Calif., September 24, 1954).   [469

...**Disputes.** Government can do a great deal to aid the settlement of labor disputes without allowing itself to be employed as an ally of either side. Its proper role in industrial strife is to encourage the process of mediation and conciliation. (State of the Union Message, Washington, D. C., February 2, 1953).   [470

...**Free.** Free labor can outwork, outproduce, outearn and outdo slave labor, whether that slave labor be located in a Nazi Germany or a Communist Russia. (As Republican Candidate for President, speech to American Federation of Labor, New York, N. Y., September 17, 1952).   [471

...**Industry.** I am in favor not of repealing, but of amending, the law. I will not support any amendments which weaken the rights of working men and women . . . I do not want arbitrary power over either labor or industry. (As Republican Candidate for President, statement on Taft-Hartley Act, October, 1952).   [472

... Private Enterprise. No group in our country is more firmly dedicated to the retention and development of our system of private enterprise than is American labor. (As President of Columbia University, speech to American Bar Association, St. Louis, Mo., September 5, 1949). [473

... Strikes. In our present world—in this kind of prolonged tension and struggle—a crippled industry or a demoralized working force could be the equivalent of a lost battle. (Speech over radio, Washington, D. C., May 19, 1953). [474

... Unions. Our truly American labor unions have helped greatly in stiffening the American worker's resistance to communism. (As Republican Candidate for President, speech to Convention of the American Federation of Labor, New York, N. Y., September 17, 1952). [475

... Unions. Today in America unions have a secure place in our industrial life. Only a handful of unreconstructed reactionaries harbor the ugly thought of breaking unions. Only a fool would try to deprive working men and women of the right to join the union of their choice. (As Republican Candidate for President, speech to Convention of the American Federation of Labor, New York, N. Y., September 17, 1952). [476

LATIN AMERICA

Our hope is that through the Organization of Pan-American States that our general attitude toward this whole business of promoting peace and friendly relations in the world will have a solid foundation and agreement among our own American States. That is, I should say, one of the cornerstones of American policy. (Press conference, February 2, 1955).   [477

The bonds among our American Republics are not merely geographic; rather they are shared principles and convictions. Together we believe in God, in the dignity and rights of man, in peace with justice, and in the right of every people to determine its own destiny. In such beliefs our friendship is rooted. (Speech over radio and television, Washington, D. C., prior to departure on South American trip, February 21, 1960).   [478

The people of Latin America know that poverty, ignorance and ill health are not inevitable. They are determined to have their resources and labors yield a better life for themselves and for their children. (Speech over radio and television, Washington, D. C., March 8, 1960).   [479

LAW

I do not believe that we can cure all of the evils in men's hearts by law. (As Republican Candidate for President, Interview in Abilene, Kans., June 1952).   [480

In a very real sense the world no longer has a choice between force and law. If civilization is to survive, it must choose the rule of law. (Statement for Law Day, April 30, 1958).   [481

The law in our times . . . does its part to build a society in which the homes of workers will be invaded neither by the sovereign's troops nor by the storms and winds of insecurity and poverty. It does this not by paternalism, welfarism and handouts but by creating a framework of fair play within which conscientious, hardworking men and women can freely obtain a just return for their efforts. (Statement for Law Day, April 30, 1958).   [482

The rule of law does more than insure freedom from high-handed action of rulers. It insures justice between man and man—however humble the one and however powerful the other. (Statement for Law Day, April 30, 1958).   [483

. . . and Order. What we have to do in America is generate a great belief in democracy. One of the things it demands is respect for law and order. (Interview, Gettysburg, Pa., November, 1966).   [484

. . . Disregard. I'm concerned about a general disregard for the moral law and the legal law in this country. A deterioration has been going on since the first World War. (Speech at Denison, Tex., high school auditorium which was renamed for him, September 1, 1965).   [485

. . . Moral. The most heartening, hopeful phenomenon in the world today is that people have experienced a great awakening. They see the evils of the past as crimes against the moral law, injuring the offender as well as the victim. They recognize that only under the rule of moral law can all of us realize our deepest and noblest aspirations. (Speech to Indian Parliament, New Delhi, India, December 10, 1959).   [486

. . . Observance. The overwhelming majority of our people in every section of the country are united in their respect for observance of the law—even in those cases where they may disagree with that law. They deplore the call of extremists to violence. (Speech from Washington, D. C., September 24, 1957).   [487

...**Politics.** Obviously, a rough equality between the two great political parties should be maintained on the bench. Thus we help assure that the judiciary will realistically appraise and apply precedent and principles in the light of current American thinking, and will never become a repository of unbalanced partisan attitudes. (Speech to American Bar Association, Philadelphia, Pa., August 24, 1955).   [488

LAWS

Laws that needlessly impose stifling controls and inflexible rules beyond the codes necessary to fair play may be necessary in a dictatorship—but in a democracy they are futile at the best and the cause of rebellion at the worst. (As president of Columbia University, speech to American Bar Association, St. Louis, Mo., September 5, 1949).   [489

LEADERS

...**Leadership.** Let us pray that leaders of both the near and distant future will be able to keep the nation strong and at peace, that they will lead us on to still higher moral standards, and that, in achieving these goals, they will maintain a reasonable balance between private and governmental responsibility. (QUOTE, January 29, 1961, in farewell State of the Union Message).   [490

LEADERSHIP

Without American leadership in the search, the pursuit of a just and enduring peace is hopeless. Nowhere in the world—outside this land—is there the richness of resources, stamina and will needed to lead what at times may be a costly and exhausting effort. (As President of Columbia University, First of a Series of Lectures Dedicated to the Cause of International Peace, Columbia University, New York, N. Y., April, 1950). [491

More benefit for America is to be found in an ounce of real leadership and honest speech than in a ton of law that fails to reflect the considered will of the vast majority. (Speech to homecoming gathering, Abilene, Kans., May 4, 1952). [492

When we, ourselves, can take honest pride in our national leadership, people in other lands will wish to share that pride. (As Republican Candidate for President, speech in San Francisco, Calif., October 8, 1952). [493

America is today the strongest, the most influential and most productive nation in the world . . . America's leadership and prestige depend, not merely upon our unmatched material progress, riches and military strength, but on how we use our power in the interests of world peace and human betterment. (Speech over radio and television, Washington, D. C., January 17, 1961). [494

. . . **Strength.** Leadership cannot be exercised by the weak. It demands strength—the strength of this great nation when its people are united . . . This spiritual and economic strength in turn must be reinforced in a still armed world by the physical strength necessary for the defense of ourselves and our friends. (Address at Columbia University, New York, N. Y., March 23, 1950).   [495

... **World.** We have accepted the burdens of world leadership with clear mind and confident heart—for we know that to strengthen other free men is to serve our own freedom and safety. (Speech over radio, Washington, D. C., August 6, 1953).   [496

LEBANON

I believe that the presence of the United States forces now being sent to Lebanon will have a stabilizing effect which will preserve the independence and integrity of Lebanon. It will also afford an increased measure of security to the thousands of Americans who reside in Lebanon. (Speech over radio, Washington, D. C., July 15, 1958).   [497

LEND-LEASE

In World War II we used a system we called lend-lease, and I heard often in my headquarters people criticize this scheme of lend-lease. I never could feel that way about it, and I will tell you why . . . It took a rifle and a man to go out and advance the cause of the Allies against the enemies we had. If the U. S. could provide merely the rifle and get someone else to carry it in order to do the work that was necessary, I was perfectly content. (As General of the Army, speech to Members of Congress, Library of Congress, Washington, D. C., February 1, 1951).   [498

LIBERTY

The fundamental principles of human liberty and free government are powerful sources of human energy, loyalty, dedication and guides to enduring success. They are mightier than armaments and armies. (Speech at Baylor University Commencement, Waco, Tex., May 25, 1956).   [499

It has long been my judgment that the real threat to liberty in this republic will not come from any sudden calculated onslaught. Rather, the threat to our liberties will be primarily found in steady erosion of self-reliant citizenship and in excessive power concentration resulting from the lodging of more and more decisions in an ever-growing federal bureaucracy. (New conference, Washington, D. C., May 10, 1962).   [500

... Independence.   America must demonstrate to the world . . . that personal liberty and national independence are not only cherished dreams; they are workable concepts. (Remarks to 1959 Washington Conference of the Advertising Councils, Washington, D. C., April 13, 1959).   [501

··M··

MAN

...Discoveries. Every discovery we have made, even the use of fire to warm our bodies, to cook our food, has also been used as one of the devastating weapons of war to bring destruction to enemies. Every single thing that man has discovered can be used for good or for evil depending upon the purpose of man. (Speech at ceremony marking the issuance of the Atoms-for-Peace postage stamp, Washington, D. C., July 27, 1955).   [502

...Nature. It is of the utmost importance then that each of us understand the true nature of the world struggle now taking place. It is not a struggle merely of economic theories, or of forms of government, or of military power. The issue is the true nature of man. (State of the Union Message, January 6, 1955).   [503

...Soul. We must seek in our churches, our schools, our homes and our daily lives the clearness of mind and strongness of heart to guard the chance to live in freedom. For this whole struggle, in the deepest sense, is waged neither for land nor for food nor for power—but for the soul of man himself. (Speech to National Junior Chamber of Commerce, Minneapolis, Minn., June 10, 1953).   [504

MEETINGS

...Summit. It is absolutely futile and, in my opinion, damaging, to attempt to hold a "summit" meeting, unless the agenda and the subjects included on it are so well prepared as to give a genuine belief that real progress—if not fixed agreement, but real progress—toward easing of tensions can be accomplished. (News conference, March 5, 1958).   [505

MIDDLE EAST

Our country supports without reservation the full sovereignty and independence of each and every nation of the Middle East. (Speech to Congress, Washington, D. C., January 5, 1957).   [506

The Middle East is the birthplace of three great religions—Moslem, Christian and Hebrew. Mecca and Jerusalem are more than places on the map. They symbolize religions which teach that the spirit has supremacy over matter and that the individual has a dignity and rights of which no despotic government can rightfully deprive him. It would be intolerable if the holy places of the Middle East should be subjected to a rule that glorifies atheistic materialism. (Speech to Congress, Washington, D. C., January 5, 1957).   [507

...Russia. The Soviet Union has nothing whatsoever to fear from the United States in the Middle East, or anywhere else in the world, so long as its rulers do not themselves first resort to aggression. (Speech to Congress, Washington, D. C., January 5, 1957).   [508

MIDDLE OF THE ROAD

The Middle of the Road is derided by all of the right and the left . . . Yet here is the truly creative area within which we may obtain agreement for constructive social action compatible with basic American principles . . . It is the area in which are rooted the hopes and allegiances of the vast majority of our people. (Speech to American Bar Association, St. Louis, Mo., September 5, 1949).   [509

People talk about the middle of the road as though it were unacceptable. . . . The middle of the road is all of the usable surface. The extremes, right and left, are in the gutters. (QUOTE, November 17, 1963, press conference).   [510

MILITARY-INDUSTRIAL COMPLEX

In the councils of government, we must guard against the acquisition of unwarranted influence, whether sought or unsought, by the military-industrial complex. The potential for the disastrous rise of misplaced power exists and will persist. (Speech over radio and television, Washington, D. C., January 17, 1961).   [511

MILITARY MIGHT

So far as we are concerned, the amassing of military might never has been—and never will be—devoted to any other end than defense and the preservation of a just peace.

(Speech over radio and television, Washington, D. C., November 7, 1957).   [512

MILITARY SERVICE

The average man benefits from military training . . . The average veteran has developed in leadership, in initiative, in mental maturity and in self-reliance by reason of his service. The medical check-up and his physical hardening incident of his duty are positive assets. (As Chief of Staff, speech to Congress of Industrial Organizations, Atlantic City, N. J., November 20, 1946).   [513

The man who today dismisses our military draft as "an incredible waste" is a man speaking incredible folly. (As Republican nominee for President, speech in Los Angeles, Calif., October 19, 1956).   [514

It is just as much of a duty to learn "how" to serve the country in case of need, as it is to serve. If you don't have men with sufficient education to know how to use or to prevent the use of nuclear weapons, then you are worse off than if you didn't have the weapons. We want a nation that is patriotic, and improving itself. The nation is made up of spiritual, intellectual, economic and military strength. We want to keep these values at a high level. (News conference, Gettysburg, Pa., November, 1966).   [515

I don't believe in finding make-work jobs for rejects—a choice of the Peace Corps, or some other Government service. What we need is good, tough, military training—and I am just as much concerned for the benefit of the youths as a whole as for the military service. (News conference, Gettysburg, Pa., November, 1966).   [516

There should be exemptions for no one. Anyone who is illiterate—we should give him additional duty and good teachers, and a year of basic education in the "three R's"—reading, writing and arithmetic. We should give physical fitness for people who are now being rejected with minor defects. (News conference, Gettysburg, Pa., November, 1966).   [517

We ought to have one year of compulsory military training for everyone—not the regular pay, just a few dollars—but one year of basic education. At age 18, this would encourage a lot of enlistments. (News conference, Gettysburg, Pa., November, 1966).   [518

MILITARY STRENGTH

So long as freedom is threatened and armaments are not controlled, it is essential for us to keep a strong military establishment ourselves and strengthen the bonds of collective security. (Speech to American Society of Newspaper Editors, Washington, D. C., April 21, 1956).   [519

We must maintain our military strength, balancing it and perfecting it in weapons and in strategy so that its sheer effectiveness will restrain any aggressor. (As Republican Nominee for President, speech over radio and television, Washington, D. C., September 19, 1956).   [520

... Peace. The tasks of building and sustaining a mighty military shield are hard, and tremendously costly. The tasks of patiently building a sound world are less costly, but even harder. (Speech to National Conference on the Foreign Aspects of National Security, Washington, D. C., February 25, 1958). [521

MISSILES

The first model of any new piece of equipment is always relatively primitive. The first sewing machine, the first typewriter, the first automobile—all left much to be desired. And even the rockets that dazzle us today will soon become the Model T's—the Tin Lizzies—of the Missile Age. (Speech over radio and television, Washington, D. C., March 16, 1959). [522

MISTAKES

To be truly good servants, we need not pretend perfection. We do make mistakes. We shall continue to make them. But to see and to acknowledge them is help to atone for them. (Speech to National Young Republican Convention, Mt. Rushmore, S. Dak., June 11, 1953). [523

I never ordered a cease-fire in a battle because some of the ammunition misfired or went bad, or some commander, including myself, may have made a mistake. (Speech over radio and television, Washington, D. C., May 14, 1957). [524

MONEY

. . . Spending. When spending the other fellow's money, we have fine self-starters—but are short on brakes! (Speech to Life Insurance Association of America, New York City, N. Y., December 9, 1964).

MONOPOLY

These believers in centralization fail to warn us that monopoly is always potentially dangerous to freedom—even when monopoly is exercised by government. (Speech at Dedication of McNary Dam, Ore., September 23, 1954).
[526

MORALE

I beg of you, as you hear us talk of morale and spirit, not to belittle those qualities. I think possibly a soldier comes to place more value on the word "morale" than most people. (As Allied Supreme Commander in Europe, views given to subcommittee of Senate Foreign Relations Committee in special hearing, Paris, France, July 9, 1951).
[527

MORAL VALUES

I deeply believe that one of the supreme hopes for the world's destiny lies in the American community; in its moral values, in its senses of order and decency, in its cooperative spirit. (Speech to Sixth National Assembly of the United Church Women, Atlantic City, N. J., October 6, 1953).
[528

··N··

NAME CALLING

I don't mind what names they call me. I remember at canning season, my mother conserved the good things of the garden—not the cockleburs and sunflowers. All I am trying to do is conserve the good things we have had all these years. (QUOTE, July 6, 1952, asked if he minded being called a political conservative). [529

NATIONAL DEFENSE

Nobody can defend another nation. The true defense of a nation must be found in its own soul, and you cannot import a soul. (As General of the Army, speech to Members of Congress, Washington, D. C., February 1, 1951). [530

A century and a half ago George Washington gave us some good advice. He said we should keep a good national defense. He also said we should not ungenerously impose upon our children the burdens which we ourselves ought to bear. I know you and I agree with Washington on these points. (Speech over radio and television, Washington, D. C., March 15, 1954). [531

NATIONAL SECURITY

I firmly believe that the only prescription for absolute security for any nation, including our own, is international understanding and co-operation. A shining example is the international boundary between us and our neighbors, north and south. (Speech to American Legion, New York, N. Y., August 29, 1947).   [532

Our national security is found in the combined moral, mental and physical strength of 140 million people, including the productivity of their factories and their farms and the skills with which they utilize their own resources. (Speech to Chamber of Commerce of the State of New York, New York, N. Y., May 7, 1948).   [533

National security requires an industrious and productive America, for here is the vital source of all our military strength. (Speech over radio, Washington, D. C., May 19, 1953).   [534

The plain truth is that security is planned, not blindly bought. It is the product of thought, and work, and our ability and readiness to bear our military burden for however long the threat to freedom persists. (Speech over radio, Washington, D. C., May 19, 1953).   [535

National security requires far more than military power. Economic and moral factors play indispensable roles. (State of the Union Message, Washington, D. C., January 10, 1957).   [536

Our national security needs encompass more than excellence and strength in our own military establishment. They include measures to build free world strength everywhere. (Message to Congress, Washington, D. C., August 8, 1960).   [537

Steadfast support of the concepts of justice, individual liberty and human dignity is as vital to our security today as are all of the destructive bombs deployed across our country and in bases abroad. (Speech at Testimonial Dinner for Sen. Everett Dirksen, Chicago, Ill., September 16, 1961).   [538

NATIONAL WELFARE

National welfare—that is, general security from the four fundamental evils of human existence: fire, famine, pestilence and war—is the business of each citizen because it is he, ultimately, who suffers or profits. Because he has made it his business, we have attained measurable success over fire, famine and pestilence. (As Chief of Staff, speech to the National Board of Fire Underwriters, New York, N. Y., May 27, 1947).   [539

NATIONALISM

Nationalism is a mighty and a relentless force. No conspiracy of power, no compulsion of arms, can stifle it forever. (Speech to Philippine Congress, Manila, June 15, 1960).
                                                                       [540

NATIONALITY

To my mind, a very young child is really of no nationality. A person achieves his nationalistic bent, let us say, through education or propaganda, but he achieves it after he is beyond, let's say, the age of mere childhood. (As General of the Army, press conference, Paris, France, June 16, 1945). [541

NATIONS

... **Co-operation.** Co-operation among us, whether it be in trade for increased prosperity or in the task of protecting our free institutions from aggression, is the common obligation of all. Unless each nation performs this task to the extent of its capacity, then none of us can long live in peace. (Speech at wreath laying ceremony, Colombus Circle, New York, N. Y., October 12, 1958). [542

... **Developing.** If we grasp this opportunity to build an age of productive partnership between the less fortunate nations and those that have already achieved a high state of economic advancement, we will make brighter the outlook for a world order based upon security, freedom, and peace. Otherwise, the outlook could be dark indeed. (State of the Union Message, Washington, D. C., January 7, 1960). [543

... **Duty.** I believe it is the duty of every nation, no matter how large or small, how weak or strong, to contribute to the wellbeing of the world community of free men. (Speech to Uruguayan Congress, Montevideo, March 2, 1960). [544

... **Economy.** It is important that we remember that what each of us decides in his own country affects the fortunes of the rest of us. Each country can render a great service to every other country by keeping its own economic house in order. (Speech to the Boards of Governors of the International Bank for Reconstruction and Development, and International Monetary Fund and the International Finance Corporation, Washington, D. C., September 23, 1957).   [545

. . . Interference. The United States has no intention of interfering in the internal affairs of any nation; by the same token we reject any attempt to impose its (the Soviet Union's) system on us or on other peoples by force or subversion. (State of the Union Message, Washington, D. C., January 7, 1960).   [546

. . . Past. Time and again governments have abused the fields of earth by staining them with blood and scarring them with the weapons of war. They have used the scientific mastery over nature to win a dominance over others—even made commerce an instrument of exploitation. (Speech to Indian Parliament, New Delhi, India, December 10, 1959). [547

. . . Policy. The prospects for peace are brightest when enlightened self-governing peoples control the policy of nations. Rulers beyond the reach of popular control are more likely to engage in reckless adventures and to raise the grim threat of war. (Speech to American Society of Newspaper Editors, Washington, D. C., April 21, 1956).   [548

. . . Political Union. We remain determined to play our part in achieving the political union of all countries so divided. But we do not intend to employ war as an instrument

138

to accomplish the world-wide political settlements to which we are dedicated and which we believe to be just. (Letter sent to Pres. Syngman Rhee of Korea, June 6, 1953). [549

... **Security.** The continuing need of all free nations today is for each to recognize clearly the essentiality of an unbreakable bond among themselves based upon a complete dedication to the principles of collective security, effective cooperation and peace with justice. (State of the Union Message, Washington, D. C., January 12, 1961). [550

... **Spirit.** The spirit of a people is not to be measured by its size or its riches or even its age. It is something that comes from the heart. (Speech to Philippine Congress, Manila, June 15, 1960). [551

... **Strength.** We live in a shrunken world, a world in which oceans are crossed in hours, a world in which a single-minded despotism menaces the scattered freedoms of scores of struggling independent nations. To insure the combined strength of friendly nations is for all of us an elementary matter of self-preservation—as elementary as having a stout militia in the days of the flintlock. (Speech to Republican National Convention, San Francisco, Calif., August 23, 1956). [552

... **Strength.** If other friendly nations are strong and free, our own strength and freedom are more secure. (Speech to Committee for International Economic Growth and Committee to Strengthen the Frontiers of Freedom, Washington, D. C., May 2, 1960). [553

...**Understanding.** If our peoples, in the months and years ahead, broaden their knowledge and their understanding of each other, as we, during this week, have broadened our knowledge of each other, further agreement between our governments may be facilitated. (Speech at Head of Government Meeting, Geneva, Switzerland, July 23, 1955). [554

...**Unity.** This nation and all nations defending freedom everywhere in the world are one in their common need and their common cause and none can sanely seek security alone. (Speech to Annual Convention of the National Junior Chamber of Commerce, Minneapolis, Minn., June 10, 1953). [555

...**Unity.** All of us have learned . . . that all free nations must stand together, or they shall fall separately. (Speech to Annual Convention of the National Junior Chamber of Commerce, Minneapolis, Minn., June 10, 1953). [556

...**Unity.** The strength of the free world lies not in cementing the free worlds into a second monolithic mass to compete with that of the Communists. It lies rather in the unity that comes of the voluntary association of nations which, however diverse, are developing their own capacities and asserting their own national destinies in a world of freedom and of mutual respect. (Speech to Republican National Convention, San Francisco, Calif., August 23, 1956). [557

...**Unity.** The partnership of our countries (Greece and U. S. A.) is a striking example of the way in which free nations working together can contribute to the peace and security of the international community. (Message to King Paul of Greece on 10th Anniversary of Greek-Turkish Aid Program, March 12, 1957).   [558

... **Unity.**   The example of Britain, of America, of Canada, and the rest of the Commonwealth, marching forward, carrying the flag of unity and co-operation, will be the keynote to that great successful future that will be ours, that will belong to our children and our grandchildren. (Speech at state dinner at White House honoring Queen Elizabeth II and Prince Philip, October 17, 1957).   [559

... **Wealthy.**   To remain secure and prosperous themselves, wealthy nations must extend the kind of co-operation to the less fortunate members that will inspire hope, confidence and progress. A rich nation can for a time, without noticeable damage to itself, pursue a course of self-indulgence, making its single goal the material ease and comfort of its own citizens . . . But the enmities it will incur, the isolation into which it will descend, and the internal moral and spiritual, economic, and political softness that will be engendered, will, in the long term, bring it to disaster. (State of the Union Message, Washington, D. C., January 7, 1960).   [560

NATURAL RESOURCES

The best natural resources program for America will not result from exclusive dependence on Federal bureaucracy. It will involve a partnership of the states and local communities, private citizens and the Federal Government, all working together. (State of the Union Message, Washington, D. C., February 2, 1953). [561

NATURE

If the peoples of the world can not only master the forces of nature but can find also the way to use them for peaceful ends, we are on the threshold of a new era. (Press release from Taipei, June 18, 1960). [562

NEAR EAST

The peoples of the Near East are not alone in their ambition for independence and development. We are living in a time when the whole world has become alive to the possibilities of modernizing their societies. (Speech to United Nations General Assembly, New York, N. Y., August 13, 1958). [563

NEGOTIATION

We will never close the door: I have assured you people, time and time again, that if there is any possible avenue, no matter how crooked, no matter how narrow, if I can discern it and it will take us toward some easing of tensions in the world, one step toward peace, I am perfectly ready to start, no matter what the difficulty is. (News conference, March 5, 1958). [564

NEWSPAPERS

I believe this: I believe that never in any great crisis of history, a continuing crisis such as was World War II, was a public so fully informed, so rapidly informed, of the facts of the conflict as was the American public in World War II, and regardless of the great services performed by the radio and other media of mass information, it was the newspapers that brought to the American public that story, the story as it occurred. (As President of Columbia University, speech to Associated Press, New York, N. Y., April 24, 1950).   [565

I would like to say to the editor of every single newspaper in the United States: You have a duty, to find the truth, and project it fearlessly, honestly, and to the utmost ability that your heart and head will allow, to every person that you can reach. (Speech to National Editorial Association, Washington, D. C., June 22, 1954).   [566

Our newspapers have traditionally been a guarantee that truth will reach every part of our own country and all the free peoples of the world. (Speech to The Associated Press, New York, N. Y., April 25, 1955).   [567

... **Reporters.**   You boys will be down there in the barn with the rest of the bulls! (QUOTE, March 28, 1954, asked by reporters where the press room would be on his Gettysburg farm).   [568

NIXON, RICHARD M.

Except for asking for such divine guidance as I may be granted, I shall make up my mind, and that will be done as soon as I have had a chance again to meet Sen. Nixon face to face and talk to him. And I must tell you that I have been deeply impressed by his sincerity, by his frankness, by his courage. (Speech in Cleveland, Ohio, September 23, 1952).   [569

I happen to be one of those people who, when I get in a fight, would rather have a courageous and honest man by my side than a whole boxcar of pussyfooters. (Speech in Cleveland, Ohio, September 23, 1952).   [570

When a man, in further answer of what he believes to be correct and right, stands up in front of all the American people and bares his soul, brings his family with him and tells the truth and brings with him every bit of evidence that he can get hold of to substantiate his story, to bare the secrets of his economic and financial life, he is a courageous man. (Speech in Cleveland, Ohio, commenting on Sen. Richard M. Nixon's radio speech, September 23, 1952).   [571

(He) was willing to undertake any chore and whatever that chore, to perform it brilliantly and in the best interests of the United States. (QUOTE, January 15, 1961, praising the outgoing Vice-President at Mr. Nixon's birthday and farewell party).   [572

I regard him still as one of the young splendid citizens in our nation and one of the great leaders of the Republican Party. (News conference, Gettysburg, Pa., May 1, 1961).
[573

(The) worst mistake (as President) was in not working harder to elect the man (Richard Nixon) I thought should be my successor. (Press conference, Europe, August, 1962).
[574

NORTH ATLANTIC TREATY ORGANIZATION

NATO should not be thought of merely as a military

alliance. NATO is a way of grouping ability—of our manhood, our resources, of our industries and our factories. (Speech at state dinner at White House honoring Queen Elizabeth II and Prince Philip, October 17, 1957).   [575

The North Atlantic Treaty Organization was created in response to a military threat. Yet NATO should not for all time be primarily a collective defense organization. We hope and believe that the time will come when its defense aspect will be minor and perhaps even unnecessary. (Speech to North Atlantic Treaty Organization Council Meeting, Paris, France, December 16, 1957).   [576

NATO has proved itself as an agency of peace. Since it came into being no further nation of Europe has been lost to Communist aggression. (Speech to North Atlantic Treaty Organization Council Meeting, Paris, France, December 16, 1957).   [577

NUCLEAR AGE

Today we are face to face with the most extraordinary physical development of all time—the application of nuclear fission and nuclear fusion to the world's armaments. These discoveries in the field of science present in themselves no threat to man. Like other scientific developments, they are susceptible to good or evil use, depending upon the intent of the individual or group possessing them. (Speech to Sixth National Assembly of the United Church Women, Atlantic City, N. J., October 6, 1953).   [578

Knowledge can give us nuclear fission; only wisdom and understanding can assure its application to human betterment rather than to human destruction. (Speech to Alumni, Faculty Members and Friends at Columbia University, New York, N. Y., May 31, 1954).   [579

To protect our nations and our peoples from the catastrophe of a nuclear holocaust, free nations must maintain countervailing military power to persuade the Communists of the futility of seeking to advance their ends through aggression. (State of the Union Message, Washington, D. C., January 6, 1955).

We are in the era of the thermonuclear bomb that can obliterate cities and can be delivered across continents. With such weapons, war has become, not just tragic, but preposterous. (Speech to Republican National Convention, San Francisco, Calif., August 23, 1956).   [581

Nuclear-tipped missiles place all of us—even in Chicago —but 30 minutes from Armageddon—tonight, every night, every hour of every day. There is no spot on earth assured of safety from obliteration. The maximum warning time is measured in minutes. (Speech at Testimonial Dinner for Sen. Everett Dirksen, Chicago, Ill., September 16, 1961).   [582

NUCLEAR MATERIALS

My country's purpose is to help us move out of this dark chamber of horrors into the light; to find a way by which the minds of men, the hopes of men, the souls of men everywhere, can move forward toward peace, and happiness and well-being. (QUOTE, December 13, 1953, speech to

United National General Assembly, proposing all atomic nations contribute nuclear materials to an international agency under United Nations sponsorship).

NUCLEAR SUBMARINES

The George Washington and her following sister ships possess a power and relative invulnerability which will make suicidal any attempt by an aggressor to attack the free world by surprise. (QUOTE, November 20, 1960, on the launching of the nuclear-powered submarine George Washington).   [584

NUCLEAR WAR

Here, on this continent, we present an example that other nations some day surely will recognize and apply in their relations with their neighbors. . . . The only alternative —the suicide of nuclear war—cannot for long be tolerated by the human race. (QUOTE, November 22, 1953, speech at Ottawa, Canada).   [585

While America must always be alert, I think it's silly to say that we can be defeated on a first-blow attack. Any nation foolish enough to launch a nuclear attack would be destroyed by our retaliatory strength. (QUOTE, September 7, 1958).   [586

NUCLEAR WEAPONS

We witness today, in the power of nuclear weapons a new and deadly dimension to the ancient horror of war. Humanity has now achieved, for the first time in its history, the power to end its history. (As Presidential Nominee of the

Republican Party, speech over radio and television, Washington, D. C., September 19, 1956). [587

In this cause of world peace, one truth must never be lost from sight: It is this: The critical issue is not a matter of testing nuclear weapons—but of preventing their use in nuclear war. (Review of country's policy on the development and testing of nuclear weapons released from White House, October 23, 1956). [588

The likelihood of any nation, possessing these great weapons of massive destruction, using them in an attack grows less, I think, every year, I believe, as their understanding of them grows, then the less the chance that they would go on an adventure that brought these things into play, because, as I see it, any such operation today is just another way of committing suicide. (Press conference, February 6, 1957). [589

·· O ··

OBSTACLES

... **Overcoming.** Free men do not lose their patience, their courage, their faith because the obstacles are mountainous, the path uncharted. Given understanding, they invariably rise to the challenge. (Speech to American Newspaper Publishers Association, New York, N. Y., April 22, 1954).

[590

OPINIONS

I welcome the opinions and counsel of others. But in the last analysis such opinions cannot legally replace my own. (Letter to Sen. Theodore F. Green, Chairman of Senate Foreign Relations Committee, October 5, 1958).   [591

OPPORTUNITY

I believe that opportunity is greater today—and I mean individual opportunity—than it has ever been at any time in our history because opportunity, regarded in the sense that Lincoln regarded it, is this: opportunity to serve the society to which you belong. And, frankly, when our democracy with its system of free enterprise is operating properly, then individual reward comes about in the measure that you render service to others. (Speech to First Columbia College Forum on Democracy, Columbia University, New York, N. Y., February 12, 1949). [592

OPTIMISTS

... Doubters. The faint-hearted and the doubters who hang back today are apt tomorrow to be trampled in the rush of progress. It has been the tough-minded optimists whom history has proved right in America. It is still true in our time. (Speech to Economic Mobilization Conference conducted by the American Management Association, New York City, N. Y., May 20, 1958). [593

ORGANIZATION OF AMERICAN STATES

In spite of inescapable human errors in our long record, the Organization of American States is a model in the practice of brotherhood among nations. (Speech to Presidents of the American Republics in Commemoration of the Congress of Panama of 1826, Panama, July 22, 1956). [594

··P··

PACIFISM

There is no greater pacifist than the regular officer. (As General of the Army, speech at Waldorf-Astoria, New York, N. Y., June 19, 1945).   [595

PARENTS

... **Children.**   Since the day of creation, the fondest hope of men and women has been to pass on to their children something better than they themselves enjoyed. That hope represents a spark of the Divine which is implanted in every human breast. (Speech to Presidents of the American Republics in Commemoration of the Congress of Panama 1826, Panama, July 22, 1956).   [596

PATRIOTISM

I have no end to serve, as I know you have no end to serve, except the good of the United States; and that is the reason I am talking here. And that is the reason I am back in uniform, and it is the reason I have the courage to appear before this body to express my convictions. (As General of the Army, Speech to Members of Congress, Washington, D. C., February 1, 1951).   [597

It isn't enough merely to say, "I love America" and to salute the flag. And to take off your hat as it goes by, and to help sing "The Star-Spangled Banner." (Speech at Dartmouth College Commencement, Hanover, N. H., June 14, 1953). [598

Of the nations of today the future will say that there were two kinds: Those that were intelligent, courageous, decisive and tireless in their support of high principles—and those that disappeared from the earth. The true patriots (give) their best to assure that our country will always be found in the first of these categories. (QUOTE, June 12, 1955, commencement address at West Point). [599

PEACE

The peace lies, when you get down to it, with all the peoples of the world, not just for the moment with a political leader. (Farewell interview to correspondents in Paris, France, June 1945). [600

As I see it, peace is an absolute necessity to this world . . . I believe that we should let no specious argument of any kind deter us from exploring every direction in which peace can be maintained. I believe we should be strong, but we should be tolerant. We should be ready to defend our rights but we should be considerate and recognize the rights of the other man. (Speech at dinner in his honor by City of New York, June 19, 1945). [601

Peace is more the product of our day-to-day living than of a spectacular program, intermittently executed. (As President of Columbia University, First of a Series of Lectures Dedicated to the Cause of International Peace, Columbia University, New York, N. Y., April 1950).   [602

The Prince of Peace said when a strong man is armed he keepeth the peace and his goods are in peace. (QUOTE, December 2, 1951, as Supreme Commander, North Atlantic Pact Nations).   [603

The course to peace is the establishment of conditions that will abolish fear and build confidence. (Speech to American Legion, New York, N. Y., August 25, 1952).   [604

Peace—either on the labor front or on the international front—cannot be legislated. It can be secured only when there is mutual respect, a will for peace and responsible, humane leadership. (As Republican Candidate for President, speech to American Federation of Labor, New York, N. Y., September 17, 1952).   [605

I should like, of course, to give you this one conviction of my own; that all men, all masses, do truly long for peace . . . It is only governments that are stupid, not the masses of people. Governments may seek for power, for the right to dominate, to extend their authority over others. Free people do not seek that. (Speech to World Christian Endeavor Convention, Washington, D. C., July 25, 1954).   [606

There is no other longing of men so universal and so indestructible as the yearning for a lasting, just and noble peace. (Speech to the Assembly of the World Council of Churches, Evanston, Ill., August 19, 1954).   [607

Let us always remember that our basic objective is peace. But in our search for peace—indeed, in order to enhance that search—we are determined to remain secure. (Speech to American Legion, Washington, D. C., August 30, 1954).   [608

The pursuit of peace is at once our religious obligation and our national policy. (Speech at American Jewish Tercentenary Dinner, New York, N. Y., October 20, 1954).
[609

But let no man think that we want peace at any price; that we shall forsake principle in resigned tolerance of obvious evil; that we may pawn our honor for transitory concession. (QUOTE, December 26, 1954, in a Christmas Message).
[610

A sound peace—with security, justice, well-being, and freedom for the people of the world—*can* be achieved, but only by patiently and thoughtfully following a hard and sure and tested road. (Speech at Head of Government meeting, Geneva, Switzerland, July 21, 1955).   [611

Success may be long in coming . . . no setback, no obstacle to progress will ever deter this government and our people from the great effort to establish a just and durable peace. (QUOTE, November 27, 1955, on Geneva Conference).   [612

No one is more aware than I that it is the young who fight the wars, and it is the young who give up years of their lives to military training and service. It is not enough that their elders promise "peace in our time": it must be peace in their time too, and in their children's time; indeed . . . there is only one real peace now, and that is peace for all time. (Speech to Republican National Convention, San Francisco, Calif., August 23, 1956).   [613

The subject you are talking about (peace), is so important that, frankly, I don't care much about where I'm working, as long as it is a convenient place, and it can be done. (News conference, March 5, 1958).   [614

The United States has pledged its national honor to work for peace. For us, this pledge is no less than a sacred obligation. It is freely—but not lightly—given to the nations of the world. (QUOTE, January 4, 1959, in Christmas message).
[615

I like to believe that people in the long run are going to do more to promote peace than are governments. Indeed, I think that people want peace so much that one of these days governments had better get out of their way and let them have it. (QUOTE, September 6, 1959, in television talk with British Prime Minister Harold Macmillan).   [616

All the mechanics for peace available to governments cannot have the force of the urge of people for peace. If we can get more contacts between people, I am quite certain that governments will be yielding to their great conviction for peace. (QUOTE, August 26, 1962, press conference, London, England).   [617

... Change. We must not think of peace as a static condition in world affairs. That is not true peace, nor in fact can any kind of peace be preserved that way. Change is a law of life, and unless there is peaceful change, there is bound to be violent change. (Speech to American Bar Association, Philadelphia, Pa., August 24, 1955). [618

... Cost. The cost of peace is something we must face boldly, fearlessly. Beyond money, it involves changes in attitudes, the renunciation of old prejudices, even the sacrifice of some seeming self-interest. (State of the Union Message, January 10, 1957). [619

... Freedom. We know that our purpose is a just and moral one, for we seek only peace with freedom and we can succeed in this great endeavor only if each and every one of us is willing to give the full measure of courage, sacrifice, work and vision not in a divided effort but working together in pursuit of our common goal. (Speech to members of the Academy of Moral and Political Sciences, of which he was made a foreign associate, Paris, France, January, 1952). [620

... Freedom. The assurance of peace in freedom is the key to betterment of peoples everywhere; and in a just peace friendship between all peoples will flourish. (Speech at Christmas Pageant of Peace, Washington, D. C., December 23, 1959). [621

... Justice. We look upon this shaken earth, and we declare our firm and fixed purpose—the building of a peace with justice in a world where moral law prevails. The building of such a peace is a bold and solemn purpose. To proclaim it is easy. To serve it will be hard. And to attain it, we must be aware of its full meaning—and ready to pay its full price. (Second Inaugural Address, January 21, 1957). [622

... **Justice.** We shall . . . never fail to take any step, at any sacrifice, which will genuinely promote the cause of peace and justice in the world. (Letter to Soviet Premier Nikita Khrushchev, July 22, 1958). [623

... **Justice.** As long as any man, any significant sector of our world, cannot enjoy the blessings of peace with justice, then indeed there is no peace anywhere. (Speech to Foreign Service Institute, June 12, 1959). [624

... **Justice.** Our children understand, as we did not in our own youthful years, the need—now approaching the absolute—for peace with justice. And so, among the things we teach to the young are such truths as the transcendent value of the individual and the dignity of all people, the futility and stupidity of war, its destructiveness of life and its degradation of human values. (QUOTE, April 3, 1960, speech at White House Conference on children and youth). [625

... **Justice.** I assure you my leaving this office will not terminate my devotion to world peace with justice. Whenever and wherever I see liberty threatened throughout this world, so long as I can speak, I shall always be on the side of freedom. (QUOTE, October 30, 1960, to Representatives of

fifteen new African Nations at White House, Washington,
D. C.). [626

... Outer Space. What the world needs today even more
than a giant leap into outer space, is a giant step toward
peace. (Speech over radio and television, Washington,
D. C., November 7, 1957). [627

... Politics. Americans must never and will never let
the issue of security and peace become a pawn in anyone's
political chess game. (QUOTE, January 26, 1958, speech to
Members of GOP at dinner in Chicago, Ill.) [628

... Positive. A positive peace is one brought about by
active work to create the living conditions, the level of education and health, the mutual understanding, and the sense of
common purpose that make possible the genuine everyday
substance of living in harmony with our neighbors. (Speech
to National Conference on the Foreign Aspects of National
Security, Washington, D. C., February 25, 1958). [629

... Security. I believe the thing that is causing us our
great problem today is the issue of real peace and security
in the world. (As Republican Candidate for President,
questioned by top political reporters, Abilene, Kans., June,
1952). [630

... Threat. A threat to peace anywhere in the world is
of concern everywhere in the world. (Letter to Pres. Jusce-
lino Kubitschek de Oliveira of Brazil, July 25, 1958). [631

... **War.** The people of America do not want war. Peace is also the deepest desire in the hearts of average men and women in every land. The tragic fact is that so many millions of those who desire peace are the regimented of the world; forced to help build and man the war machines of dictators. (As Republican Candidate for President, speech in Philadelphia, Pa., September 4, 1952).   [632

... **War.** Mankind wants peace because the fruits of peace are manifold and rich, particularly in this atomic age; because war could be the extinction of man's deepest hope, and because atomic war could be race suicide. (Speech to American Bar Association, Philadelphia, Pa., August 24, 1955).   [633

... **War.** If men can develop weapons that are so terrifying as to make the thought of global war include almost a sentence for suicide, you would think that man's intelligence and his comprehension . . . would include also his ability to find a peaceful solution. (Press conference, Washington, D. C., November 14, 1956).   [634

... **War.** This I believe deeply: if we will but hold fast in our struggle for lasting peace, we shall, in coming years, find full justification for confidence that war will not occur and that this wearisome and dangerous armaments burden will be lifted from the shoulders of a grateful humanity. (Speech to American Society of Newspaper Editors and International Press Institute, Washington, D. C., April 17, 1958).   [635

... War. The quest for peace is the imperative of our time. War has become preposterous. And maintaining armaments is consuming resources which, if constructively used, could bring forth a new era of benefit for all mankind. (Speech to Chilean Congress, Santiago, March 1, 1960).
[636

PEOPLE-TO-PEOPLE PROGRAM

Today's announcement by the President of my connection with the People-to-People movement is gratifying. I will be delighted if I can do anything to further the work of the many thousands who are engaged in this program. (QUOTE, November 19, 1961, accepting chairmanship of board of trustees of People-to-People Program).   [637

PEOPLE

... Understanding. People are what count. A sympathetic understanding of the aspirations, the hopes and fears, the traditions and prides of other peoples and nations, is essential to the promotion of mutual prosperity and peace. (Speech at Baylor University Commencement, Waco, Tex., May 25, 1956).   [638

PERIL

We live . . . not in an instant of peril but in an age of peril—a time of tension and of watchfulness. The defense against this peril, then, must be carefully planned and steadfastly maintained . . . It cannot be a thing of frenzies and alarms. It must be a thing of thought and of order and of efficiency. (Speech to National Junior Chamber of Commerce, Minneapolis, Minn., June 10, 1953).   [639

We live in a land of plenty, but rarely has this earth known such peril as today. (Second Inaugural Address, Washington, D. C., January 21, 1957).   [640

PESSIMISM

Pessimism never won any battle, whether it was in peace or it was in war. (Speech over radio and television, July 15, 1955).   [641

Just as Job had his boils, so we have a cult of professional pessimists who, taking counsel of their fears, continually mouth the allegation that America has become a second rate military power. (Speech to Republican National Convention, Chicago, Ill., July 26, 1960).   [642

PHILANTHROPY

The American people accept as a clear responsibility the combating of privation and suffering. The growth in private philanthropic contributions in the past ten years has exceeded both the rate of growth of our population and personal income. Another amazing fact is that in this year 1960, over 45 million Americans will lend their time and talents in raising over nine billion for philanthropic causes. (QUOTE, November 13, 1960, speech to National Conference of Catholic Charities).   [643

POLITICAL DEBTS

I have no political debts. Now of course, when I say this I must ask you to make this one exception. One delegate, from my mother's home state, Virginia, brought me a fine-looking ham—now what I owe for that I'm not sure. (As Candidate for Republican nomination for President, speech in Detroit, Mich., June 14, 1952).   [644

POLITICAL LEADERSHIP

When it comes to a really critical matter like political leadership, we recall a fact that all of us have seen in our daily lives; the longest lectures almost always come from those with least experience. (QUOTE, October 7, 1956, speech at Lexington, Ky.).   [645

POLITICAL PARTIES

I would not have all these people as friends if I allied myself with one political party. (QUOTE, February 19, 1950, as President of Columbia University).   [646

Political health is endangered if one party, by whatever means, becomes permanently or too long entrenched in power. The almost inevitable consequences are graft and incompetence in remote and even in prominent places in government. (Speech to homecoming gathering, Abilene, Kans., May 4, 1952).   [647

We see our party not as an end in itself but as a magnificent means—a means through which countless thousands of devoted citizens can co-operate in the conquering of problems that beset free men everywhere. (Speech to Republican Party, Boston, Mass., September 21, 1953).   [648

It is one of the functions of a political party to develop and articulate basic convictions, so that its specific governmental actions will have the direction of well-understood principles.

(Speech to Republican Women's National Conference, Washington, D. C., March 18, 1958).   [649

Indeed, the greatest service our own or any political party can render the American people is to be a trustworthy vehicle for strengthening freedom in a world at peace. (Speech at Republican Congressional Testimonial Dinner, Washington, D. C., June 1, 1961).   [650

If we have a rough equality between our two political parties, then anyone attempting to go to extremes is going to be blocked. But if we don't have balance in our political system, if the party in power stays in power too long—who is there to stop its excesses? (Interview, Gettysburg, Pa., November, 1966).   [651

We are tending too much toward a one-party system in the United States. We are too close to a monopoly of political power in this country. (Interview, Gettysburg, Pa., November, 1966).   [652

...**Democratic.** The Democrat Party is not one—but two—political parties with the same name. They unite only once every two years—to wage political campaigns. (Speech at Los Angeles, Calif., October 20, 1958).   [653

...**Republican.** The noble service to which we Republicans summon all Americans is not only for one campaign or for one election. Our summons is to a lifetime enrollment. And our party shall always remain committed to a more secure, a brighter and an even better future for all our people. (As Republican Candidate for President, speech to Republican National Convention, Chicago, Ill., July 11, 1952).   [654

... **Republican.** The living definition of this (Republican) party, at this moment in our history, is not to be found in the fine print of a legislative record, nor beneath the dust of our historic archives. It can only be found in our own hearts and minds. Born of change—born to change—this party is and it will be what we make it. (Speech to Republican Party, Boston, Mass., September 21, 1953).   [655

... **Republican.** We (Republican party) believe that there is no cleverness of phrase that can cover shallowness of thought . . . We are the political captives of no class or section or interest of our country—and we are the prisoners of no static political or economic dogmas ruling our decisions. (Speech to Republican Party, Boston, Mass., September 21, 1953).   [656

... **Republican.** We don't believe for a minute that the Republican party is so lacking in inspiration, high quality personnel and leadership that we are dependent on one man . . . Humans are frail—and they are mortal. You never pin your flag so tightly to one mast that if a ship sinks you cannot rip it off and nail it to another. (QUOTE, September 18, 1955).   [657

... **Republican.** You will find me standing beside you, doing my very best for every member of our Grand Old

Party who carries forward the never-ending fight for peace, for security, for sound, sane and progressive government in America. (QUOTE, May 11, 1958, speech at dinner honoring Republican Members of Congress).   [658

... **Republican.**   We Republicans do not change our ideals, our aspirations of our programs, just because the other party is temporarily in power. We continue to stand for what we believe is wise and sound; we continue to fight against the unwise and the unsound. (Speech at Republican Congressional Testimonial Dinner, Washington, D. C., June 1, 1961).   [659

... **Republican.**   The Republicans have let their bill of fare get dusty. What is needed is to dust off the goods and clean up the store. (Speech to some 60 top GOP leaders and candidates, Gettysburg, Pa., July, 1962).   [660

... **Republican.**   I am dedicated to the purposes of this (Republican) party. I am jealous of its good name . . . For the good of America, Republicans must be restored in great numbers to controlling positions at all governmental levels, including the highest—the Presidency of the United States. (Speech to Republican National Convention, San Francisco, Calif., July 15, 1964).   [661

... **Republican.**   Our (Republican) party, let us never forget, was born out of protest against a supreme indignity to mankind—slavery—the story of which is found on the darkest pages of America's history, both North and South, which persisted as a social cancer even in this land of liberty until Abraham Lincoln eliminated it a century ago, supported by our party, which he led. (Speech to Republican National Convention, San Francisco, Calif., July 15, 1964).   [662

POLITICIANS

...**Reporters.** I think too often politicans look into a looking glass instead of through a window. I really believe you reporters are better judges of interests, capacities and the kind of things we are trying to do, than is some politician who, looking in the glass, sees only reflections of doubt and fear and the kind of confusion he often tries to create. (QUOTE, December 19, 1954, press conference).   [663

POLITICS

I want nothing to do with politics but that doesn't mean that I have to keep my mouth shut. (Press conference, December, 1949).   [664

No American can stand to one side while his country becomes the prey of fearmongers, quack doctors and barefaced looters. He doesn't twiddle his thumbs while his garden is wrecked by a crowd of vandals and his house is invaded by a gang of robbers. He goes into action. When the same sort of thing happens to his country, an American goes into action by getting into politics—fast and hard. (As Republican Candidate for President, speech in Indianapolis, Ind., September 9, 1952).   [665

When politics becomes the monopoly of the few and ceases to be the business of every citizen, the result is government by bureaucrats, by cronies and by machines. (As Republican Candidate for President, speech in Indianapolis, Ind., September 9, 1952).   [666

We nations of America do more than enjoy a political system constructed for ourselves. We are custodians of a way of life that can be instructive for all mankind. (Speech to Pan American Union, Washington, D. C., April 12, 1953).
                                                                        [667

The strength of America's political life depends not upon the size of political promises but the integrity of political purposes. (Speech over radio and television, Portland, Ore., October 18, 1956).   [668

I do not believe that any political campaign justifies the declaration of a moratorium on common sense. (As Republican Nominee for President, speech in Los Angeles, Calif., October 19, 1956).   [669

There is no individual who has been in political life for five minutes who has not felt at times discouragement and disappointment. (Speech to Republican National Convention, Chicago, Ill., July 26, 1960).   [670

Political labels will not influence thinking citizens. (Speech at Testimonial Dinner for Sen. Everett Dirksen, Chicago, Ill., September 16, 1961).   [671

... **Bipartisan.** I'm a bipartisan when I'm in the minority. (QUOTE, April 10, 1955).   [672

... Prejudice. Success or failure in all we hope to accomplish in attaining a peaceful world may well hinge upon our success in eliminating politics and prejudice from our nation's efforts toward this goal. (Speech to American Legion, Washington, D. C., August 30, 1954). [673

... Two-Party. Essential to America's political health today is a genuine two-party system. No other device in our particular form of government can be so effective in preserving the best of the past, in testing the new of the present, in deciding upon the possible of the future. (Speech to homecoming gathering, Abilene, Kans., May 4, 1952). [674

POPULATION

Our population is burgeoning at a rate of 3 million Americans a year. That is equivalent to adding a Kentucky to the Union every twelve months. (Speech to Economic Mobilization Conference conducted by the American Management Association, New York City, N. Y., May 20, 1958). [675

POVERTY

Abject poverty blinds men's eyes to the beauty of freedom's ideals. (Speech to American Society of Newspaper Editors, Washington, D. C., April 21, 1956). [676

In our age, for the first time in history, dreams of a better material life have become everyday hopes among millions accustomed to poverty. And for the first time in history, the aim of fostering higher living standards has become a central concern of governments everywhere and of the international community. (Speech to Boards of Governors of the International Bank for Reconstruction and Development, the International Monetary Fund and the International Finance Corporation, Washington, D. C., September 23, 1957). [677

We are getting the feeling today that we are not just taking care of the needy, but that we are acting unwisely to the extent that we are actually using the Federal Treasury to encourage and reward laziness and malingering. I would like to see more efficiency in determining who actually are the needy, and who it is that just wants to get an easier living. (Interview, Gettysburg, Pa., November, 1966). [678

... **Ignorance.** By helping eliminate poverty and ignorance, we can take another step in progress toward peace. (Speech at Head of Government Meeting, Geneva, Switzerland, July 22, 1955). [679

PRAYER

... **Inauguration.** Almighty God, as we stand here at this moment my future associates in the executive branch of government join me in beseeching that Thou will make full and complete our dedication to the service of the people in this throng, and their fellow citizens everywhere. Give us, we pray, the power to discern clearly right from wrong, and allow all our words and actions to be governed thereby, and by the laws of this land. Especially we pray that our concern shall be for all the people regardless of station, race, or calling. May cooperation be permitted and be the mutual aim of those who, under the concepts of our Constitution, hold to differing political faiths; so that all may work for the

good of our beloved country and Thy glory. (First Inaugural
Address, January 20, 1953).   [680

PREJUDICE

It is not for any man to say today that any of us have
erased from our hearts the last vestiges of prejudice. That is
not true. We are fallible people and although we may have
been created in the image of our Maker, we certainly have
not, at this time of world development, attained to that
spiritual perfection that we can claim the virtue that we
know that Creator possesses. But we can strive toward it, and
what I am trying to say, is: the virtue is in the striving.
(Speech in New York City, N. Y., September 25, 1949).
                                                        [681

PRESENT

...Future. Neither a wise man nor a brave man lies
down on the tracks of history to wait for the train of the
future to run over him. (As Republican Candidate for
President, speech in Cincinnati, Ohio, September 22, 1952).
                                                        [682

...Future. As we peer into society's future, we—you
and I, and our Government—must avoid the impulse to live
only for today, plundering for our own ease and convenience, the precious resources of tomorrow. We cannot mortgage the material assets of our grandchildren without risking
the loss also of their political and spiritual heritage. We want
democracy to survive for all generations to come, not to
become the insolvent phantom of tomorrow. (Speech over
radio and television, January 17, 1961).   [683

PRESIDENCY

My role may have changed but I have not changed. All my life I have said what I meant, and meant what I said. No one will change that. All my life I had a deep and fundamental faith in my country, in its people, in its principles and in its spiritual value. No one will change that. (As Republican Candidate for President, speech to American Federation of Labor, New York, N. Y., September 17, 1952).   [684

You know there is one thing about being President, nobody can tell you when to sit down. (Speech to forty-fifth Annual Governors' Conference, Seattle, Wash., August 4, 1953).   [685

I would say that the Presidency is probably the most taxing job, as far as tiring of the mind and spirit; but it has also, as I have said before, its inspirations. (QUOTE, January 15, 1956, news conference, Key West, Fla.)   [686

The first duty of a President is to discharge to the limit of his ability the responsibilities of his office. On the record are the aims, the efforts, the accomplishments and the plans for the future of this Administration. Those facts constitute my personal platform. (Speech over radio and television, Washington, D. C., February 29, 1956).   [687

The duties of the President are essentially endless. No daily schedule of appointments can give a full timetable, or even a faint indication of the President's responsibilities.

(Speech over radio and television, Washington, D. C., February 29, 1956).   [688

I shall do all I can, as one human working with other humans, to push toward peace, toward freedom, toward dignity and a worthy future for every man and woman and child in the world. (Speech to Indian Parliament, New Delhi, India, December 10, 1959).   [689

I believe that the problem of the Presidency is rarely an inadequacy of power. Ordinarily, the problem is to use the already enormous power of the Presidency judiciously, temperately and wisely. (News Conference, Washington, D. C., May 10, 1962).   [690

...Federal Courts. The very basis of our individual rights and freedoms rests upon the certainty that the President and the Executive Branch of Government will support and insure the carrying out of the decisions of the Federal Courts, even, when necessary, with all the means at the President's command. Unless the President did so, anarchy would result. (Speech from the White House, Washington, D. C., September 24, 1957).   [691

...Nomination. There's no use denying that I'll fly to the moon because I couldn't if I wanted to. The same goes for politics. (Questioned as to whether he would run for President at homecoming celebrations, Abilene, Kans., June 1945).   [692

...Nomination. I am confident of my own physical strength to meet all the responsibilities of the Presidency, today and in the years just ahead. If I were not so convinced, I would never have accepted renomination to this office. (As Presidential Nominee of the Republican Party, speech over radio and television, Washington, D. C., September 19, 1956).   [693

PRESIDENT

... **Congress.** I am not unique as a President in having worked with a Congress controlled by the opposition party —except that no other President ever did it for quite so long. Yet in both personal and official relationships we have weathered the storms of the past five years. For this I am deeply grateful. (State of the Union Message, Washington, D. C., January 7, 1960).   [694

... **Politics.** Most Americans would agree with me that it is not appropriate for the President of the United States to indulge incessantly in partisan political activity—every day on every possible occasion . . . Yet all Americans also have the deep conviction that representative government requires a healthy two-party system. In this sense, the responsibility of the President as party leader is recognized as an inescapable duty, essential to democracy itself. (Speech to National Young Republican Convention, Mt. Rushmore, S. Dak., June 11, 1953).   [695

... **Support.** All of us have our rights to decide whether or not we think operations of the past have been well conducted. But, when in time of crisis like this, everybody in the United States has to support the President of the United States, and that is what I am going to do. (Remarks after visiting Pres. Johnson at Bethesda Naval Hospital, Md., November 17, 1966).   [696

PRESIDENTIAL ELECTION

Under no circumstances will I ask for relief from this assignment (Supreme Commander NATO) in order to seek nomination to political office and I shall not participate in the pre-convention activities of those who may have such an intention with respect to me. (Statement regarding his political course, January 1952).   [697

I have never asked a single person to place me first in his preference list, and I never shall. (As Candidate for Republican Nomination for President, speech in Detroit, Mich., June 14, 1952).   [698

PRESIDENTIAL SUCCESSION

We are not trying to rewrite the Constitution. We are trying just to say that we are trying to carry out what normal humans of good faith having some confidence in each other would do in accordance with the language of the Constitution. (News conference, March 5, 1958).   [699

I believe that we should re-examine the line of (Presidential) succession with a view to providing the least disrupting transition of the Presidential power. (QUOTE, December 15, 1963).   [700

PRICE CONTROL

If we are going to live as a free people, we must not be a controlled people, and we must not start controlling prices in

times of peace. (Remarks to group of Business Magazine
Editors, Washington, D. C., June 4, 1959).   [701

PRINTING PRESS

No single technological development in all history did
more to advance the culture of the world than the invention
of the printing press. (Address to Argentine Congress, Bue-
nos Aires, February 26, 1960).   [702

PRIVILEGES

... **Principles.** We must be willing, individually and as
a Nation, to accept whatever sacrifices may be required of us.
A people that values its privileges above its principles
soon loses both. (First Inaugural Address, January 20,
1953).   [703

PROBLEMS

The problems of America are the family problems multiplied a million fold. (Speech over radio and television,
Washington, D. C., April 5, 1954).   [704

... **Solving.** We cannot expect here, in the few hours of
a few days, to solve all the problems of all the world that
need to be solved. (Speech at Head of Government Meeting, Geneva, Switzerland, July 18, 1955).   [705

... **Solving.** I have one yardstick by which I test every
major problem—and that yardstick is: is it good for America? (Speech over radio, Washington, D. C., April 16,
1956).   [706

... **Solving.** We need to pursue every possible avenue that can bring people together as friends and coworkers seeking solutions to their common problems. (Speech to foreign educators participating in the International Teacher Development Program, Washington, D. C., September 16, 1959).   [707

PRODUCTION

With wise management of the national household, our country can within a decade increase its production from the current annual level of about 460 billion dollars to 500 billion, or more, expressed in dollars of the same buying power. (Letter sent to Congress with Economic Report, January 20, 1955).   [708

PRODUCTIVITY

Upon the productive might of the individual American depend the wages, the diet, the health, the homes of millions of families. Upon this productive might depends even more—the preservation of freedom itself in this, its age of greatest peril. (Speech over radio, Washington, D. C., August 6, 1953).   [709

PROFESSORS

Professors must come out of their ivory towers to help solve the difficult economic, social and political problems of the day. These people possess some of the best brains in the country. It is their duty to find the answers, based on logic and scholarship, in an atmosphere removed from prejudice, ignorance and political aspirations. (QUOTE, August 27, 1950, as President of Columbia University).   [710

PROGRESS

Achievement and progress can not be created for our people; they can only be created by our people. (Speech to Economic Mobilization Conference conducted by the American Management Association, New York City, N. Y., May 20, 1958). [711

We must meet the world challenge and at the same time permit no stagnation in America. Stagnation we cannot afford. Unless we progress, we regress. (State of the Union Message, January 9, 1959). [712

PROPAGANDA

We must preach, demonstrate and tirelessly sell the vitality and value of freedom in the world. Nothing is more dangerous to our cause than to expect America's message to be heard if we don't bother to tell it. (Speech to American Legion, Washington, D. C., August 30, 1954). [713

For every spokesman of freedom that we assign to the struggle for men's minds and hearts, the Communists assign scores; for every dollar we spend for information purposes, they spend fifty in opposition; for every word we utter in the cause of liberty and faith, they utter thousands to extol their system and to degrade and defame the values of the free. (Speech to American Legion, Washington, D. C., August 30, 1954). [714

PROSPERITY

This Administration believes that no American—no one group of Americans—can truly prosper unless all Americans prosper. We are one family made up of millions of Americans with the same hopes for a full and happy life. We must not become a nation divided into factions, or special groups and hostile cliques. (Speech over radio, Washington, D. C., January 4, 1954).   [715

We can never pep-talk our way to prosperity. (Speech to Economic Mobilization Conference conducted by the American Management Association, New York City, N. Y., May 20, 1958).   [716

...**Individuals.** Lasting prosperity of the Nation depends far more on what individuals do for themselves than on what the Federal Government does or can do for them. (Letter to Congress with Economic Report, January 24, 1956).   [717

PUBLIC OPINION

You have often heard it said, I think that public opinion wins wars. And I would say with respect to that, in adapting it to the terms of peace, that only an informed public opinion can win the peace. (As President of Columbia University, speech to Associated Press, New York, N. Y., April 24, 1950).   [718

If our economy is to develop properly . . . we must have an enlightened, informed public opinion. In any free country, the great motivation which makes the whole thing operate, is public opinion. If that opinion is well-informed respecting the vital issues of our day, then Congress and the Executive, heedful of that kind of opinion, are going to act with more wisdom than they otherwise might if they were thinking only of the next election. (Remarks to group of Business Magazine Editors, Washington, D. C., June 4, 1959).   [719

The U. S. is a government in which public opinion is the motivating force behind everything that happens. (Speech to the Chamber of Commerce of the United States, Washington, D. C., May 2, 1960).   [720

PUBLIC WORKS

I am determined not to get bogged down in a slow-starting, emergency public works program, which would provide a minimum of jobs now and a maximum of budgetary headaches in the years ahead. (Speech to the Economic Mobilization Conference conducted by the American Management Association, New York City, N. Y., May 20, 1958).   [721

··R··

RACE RELATIONS

I think there ought to be biracial conferences in every city and every community of the South, which would be much better than trying to get up here and direct every single thing from Washington. I am one of those people that believes there is too much interference in our private affairs and, you might say, personal lives already. And I would like to diminish rather than increase it. (News conference, Washington, D. C., March 16, 1960).   [722

RECOGNITION

No matter how unworthy any individual may be, no matter how much he may appreciate his own shortcomings in attaining the ideas in which he himself believes, it is still a moment of the most intense satisfaction when some organization standing as it does . . . for the great human rights, chooses to present its annual emblem to that individual. (Speech after receiving the America's Democratic Legacy Award at annual dinner of the Anti-Defamation League of B'nai B'rith, Washington, D. C., November 23, 1953). [723

RELIGION

Religion nurtures men of faith, men of hope, men of love; such men are needed in the building of a new world reflecting the glory of God. (As Chief of Staff, Speech to 16th Annual Convention of the Chaplains' Association of Army and Navy, Washington, D. C., October 23, 1946).   [724

We are essentially a religious people. We are not merely religious by tradition. We are inclined more today than ever to see the value of religion as a practical force in our affairs. Contrary to what many people think, the percentage of our population belonging to churches steadily increases. In a hundred years, that percentage has multiplied more than three times. (Speech to the Assembly of the World Council of Churches, Evanston, Ill., August 19, 1954).   [725

... **Morality.** The more vigorous our religious institutions, the greater possibility that the voice of morality will be heard in widening areas of public life and in the consideration of national and international problems. (Message to Dr. Maurice N. Eisendrath of the Union of American Hebrew Congregations, February 12, 1955).   [726

REPUBLICANISM

Never-failing concern for every human being in America, no matter what his religion or the color of his skin. That, as I see it, is Republicanism. (QUOTE, June 30, 1957, speech to Young Republican National Federation).   [727

RESOURCES

At the foundation of our economic growth are the raw materials and energy produced from our minerals and fuels, lands and forests, and water resources. With respect to them, I believe that the nation must adhere to three fundamental policies: first, to develop, wisely use and to conserve basic resources from generation to generation; second, to follow the historic pattern of developing these resources primarily by private citizens under fair provisions of law, including restraints for proper conservation; and third, to treat resource development as a partnership undertaking—a partnership in which the participation of private citizens and State and local governments is as necessary as is federal participation. (State of the Union Message, Washington, D. C., January 6, 1955). [728

RESPONSIBILITY

Of course, each of us has his moments of discouragement. But is there anyone who has ever carried any responsibility who has not on many occasions during his life, or at least once in his life, said, "Is it all worth while?" (As Allied Supreme Commander in Europe, views given to subcommittee of Senate Foreign Relations Committee, Paris, France, July 22, 1951). [729

I have great responsibility to a lot of people who, rightly or wrongly, believe that I can be of service to the United States in the political world. I am not going to let those people down. (As Republican Candidate for President, press conference, Abilene, Kans., June 1952). [730

... **Individual.** When freedom is threatened from without, it is more than ever necessary that we, here at home, watch the line that separates governmental from individual responsibility. (As President of Columbia University, speech to New York Herald Tribune Forum, New York, N. Y., October 25, 1949).   [731

RUSSIA

...**Aid.** The Soviet Union wants to gain economic and ultimately political, control of the countries she pretends to help. We, on the other hand, want these countries to stand on their own feet as proud, robust friends and partners with whom we can live in mutual respect. (Speech to the National Conference on the Foreign Aspects of National Security, Washington, D. C., February 25, 1958).   [732

...**America.** I see nothing in the future that would prevent Russia and the United States from being the closest possible friends. (As General of the Army, press conference, Moscow, August 14, 1945).   [733

...**America.** I would not wish to participate in a mere gesture, which, in present circumstances, might convey a thoroughly misleading and unfortunate impression to the peoples of the world. (QUOTE, October 9, 1960, on meeting with Soviet Premier Nikita S. Khrushchev).   [734

...**Russians.** I have found the individual Russian one of the friendliest persons in the world. He likes to talk with us, laugh with us. He loves to laugh, and I have talked to many British officers and they find him the same way. He likes to see the humor of life. (As General of the Army, press conference, Paris, France, June 16, 1945).   [735

... **War.** If they (the Russians) declared war now, they are really fools. They cannot win on the global picture instantly and quickly by a complete knockout. They would face a long, bitter struggle of attrition against the United States. (QUOTE, March 18, 1951, as Supreme Commander of North Atlantic Forces). [736

·· S ··

SACRIFICE

If every American sacrifice is not matched by equal sacrifices by the people and governments of the European democracies, we are not going to win this security. (QUOTE, January 14, 1951, as Supreme Commander of North Atlantic Forces).   [737

SATISFACTION

... **Progress.** If I found a satisfied soldier, I would fire him. Because we are never going to have the progress; we are never going to do as well as we can. There is no human being that actually does his best. He just approaches it; and, as he approaches it, why, he becomes something really fine. But we never really succeed. (As Allied Supreme Commander in Europe, views given to subcommittee of Senate Foreign Relations Committee, Paris, France, July 9, 1951).   [738

SCHOLARS

... **Domination.** The prospect of domination of the nation's scholars by Federal employment, project allocations and the power of money is ever present, and is gravely to be regarded. (Speech over radio and television, Washington, D. C., January 17, 1961).   [739

SCHOOLS

Those who shout loudest about "the Reds in our schools" have done little to inform themselves at first-hand or to make sure that we had good schools. (QUOTE, February 13, 1949, as President of Columbia University, letter to university alumni).   [740

A distinguishing characteristic of our nation—and a great strength—is the development of our institutions within the concept of individual worth and dignity. Our schools are among the guardians of that principle. (Message to Congress on education, February 8, 1955).   [741

...Government Aid.   It is my firm belief that there should be Federal help to provide stimulus to correct an emergency situation . . . Federal help in building schools will not mean federal control. After these new schools are built, after the bricks are laid and the mortar is dry, the federal mission will be completed. All control and use of those schools will be in the hands of the states and of the localities. (Speech to National Education Association, Washington, D. C., April 4, 1957).   [742

...Integration.   During the past several years, many communities in our Southern States have instituted public school plans for gradual progress in the enrollment and attendance of school children of all races in order to bring themselves into compliance with the law of the land. They thus demonstrated to the world that we are a nation in which laws, not men, are supreme. (Speech from the White House, Washington, D. C., September, 24, 1957).   [743

... **International.** However high the price of a school for global understanding might be, it would still be a minute fraction of the moneys now spent by governments on defense against global war. (QUOTE, August 12, 1962, speech in Stockholm, proposing an international school to study world issues).   [744

... **Teachers.** Any man who underestimates the importance of the American teacher in world affairs is misleading himself. Under our system, high governmental policy expresses the considered will of the people, and the will of the people, in the last analysis, is compounded out of the convictions, the idealisms, the purposes fostered in the classrooms of the nation's schools. (As President of Columbia University, First of a Series of Lectures Dedicated to the Cause of International Peace, Columbia University, New York, N. Y., April, 1950).   [745

SCIENCE

According to my scientific friends, one of our greatest and most glaring deficiencies is the failure of us in this country to give high priority enough to scientific education and to the place of science in our national life. (Speech over radio and television, Washington, D. C., November 7, 1957).   [746

... **Intellect.** Now, only a year ago the hydrogen bomb was exploded in the Pacific. Last month another series of these was undertaken. Now, this transfer of power, this increase of power from the mere musket and the little cannon all the way to the hydrogen bomb in a single lifetime is indicative of things that happened to us. They rather indicate how far the advances of science have out-raced our social consciousness, how much more we have developed scientifically than we are capable of handling emotionally and intellectually. (Speech over radio and television, Washington, D. C., April 5, 1954).   [747

SCIENTISTS

You cannot say to a research worker, "Your salary is tripled; get busy now and produce three times as many basic discoveries." But wise investment in such facilities as laboratories and high-energy accelerators can greatly increase the efficiency of our scientists. (Speech in Oklahoma City, Okla., November 13, 1957).   [748

Today the solitary inventor, tinkering in his shop, has been overshadowed by task forces of scientists, in laboratories and testing fields. (Speech over radio and television, Washington, D. C., January 17, 1961).   [749

...Peace. But surely, even the men in the Kremlin must realize that before all mankind now lies a grand prospect of a far better life for every one. Its achievement requires only that the scientists of every nation concentrate on the means to a plentiful life rather than on the tools of sudden death; that the millions now under arms be released to fruitful work; that industries of war be converted to the production of useful goods. We have sought and will seek to make this prospect a reality. (Speech to Alumni, Faculty

Members and Friends, Columbia University, New York, N. Y., May 31, 1954). [750

SECRECY

In an age of rapidly developing technology, secrecy is not only an anachronism—it is downright dangerous. (Speech to Fifteenth General Assembly of the United Nations, New York, N. Y., September 22, 1960). [751

SECRETARY OF STATE

The Secretary of State of the U. S. is the greatest and most important job in the world. (Press conference, Washington, D. C., January 30, 1957). [752

SECURITY

In these times we hear so much of security, security for everything we do . . . You have come to the wrong place if you are seeking complete fulfillment of any ambition that deals with perfect security . . . I should think that the best example of it would be a man serving a lifetime in a Federal prison. (Speech at Columbia University, New York, N. Y., September 28, 1949). [753

True security never rests upon the shoulders of men denied a decent present and the hope of a better future. (As Supreme Commander in Europe, speech to English Speaking Union, London, England, July 3, 1951). [754

. . . Peace. In the last analysis, we can have positive security only through positive peace. (Speech to National

Conference on the Foreign Aspects of National Security, Washington, D. C., February 25, 1958).   [755

... **Peace.** Our hopes for permanent security and peace today is not in fortifications and walls. It is in the hearts and minds and unity of purpose of the people whose ideals we share throughout the free world. (Speech to National Conference on the Foreign Aspects of National Security, Washington, D. C., February 25, 1958).   [755

SELFISH GAIN

We shall never acquiesce in the enslavement of any people in order to purchase fancied gain for ourselves. (State of the Union Message, Washington, D. C., February 2, 1953).   [757

SELFISHNESS

There is no room in America for narrow selfishness, either personal or collective. (Speech to United States Chamber of Commerce, Washington, D. C., April 27, 1959).   [758

SERVICE

There is nothing in Lincoln's life or in Lincoln's writings that could lead any of us to believe that he recognized or believed that he himself was a source of power. He was a director of power, a man who might give it its trend to go somewhere, but he had no ambition to associate the source of power with himself and, thereby, rule others. He served others. That, to me, is the true essence of liberty and of freedom. (Speech to First Columbia College Forum on Democracy, Columbia University, New York, N. Y., February 12, 1949). [759

Almost everywhere you turn in this country, you will find a confluence of religious forces producing a person or an institution with service to others as an objective. (Speech to the Assembly of the World Council of Churches, Evanston, Ill., August 19, 1954). [760

This country has long understood that by helping other peoples to a better understanding and practice of representative government, we strengthen both them and ourselves. The same truth applies to the economic field. We strengthen other peoples and ourselves when we help them to understand the workings of a free economy, to improve their own standards of living, and to join with us in world trade that serves to unite us all. (Speech telephoned from Gettysburg, Pa. to AFL-CIO Convention, New York, N. Y., December 5, 1955). [761

SLAVERY

The grave mistake of Hitler's strategy is that he was obliged to reduce to slavery those whom he had conquered so that he could continue to run his economic machine towards the goal which he believed to be victory. (As General of the Army, Speech at Hotel de Ville, Paris, France, June 14, 1945). [762

SMUGNESS

In our time of prosperity and progress, one thing we must always be on guard against is smugness. (Speech to Republican National Convention, San Francisco, Calif., August 23, 1956).   [763

SOCIAL EVOLUTION

Each period of history brings its call for supreme human effort. At times in the past it took the form of war. Today it takes the form of social evolution or revolution. (News conference, U. S. Naval Base, Newport, R. I., July 11, 1960).   [764

SOCIALISM

...Dictatorship. Beyond pure Socialism I believe lies pure dictatorship, and you can't escape it. (As Republican Candidate for President, news conference, Abilene, Kans., June, 1952).   [765

SOCIAL SECURITY

We must improve it and extend it . . . Security for old age, unemployment insurance, care for dependent children and widows . . . are moral obligations. But they also are a sound investment in a sounder America. (As Republican Candidate for President, statement on Social Security, October, 1952).   [766

SOLDIERS

I do not differentiate among soldiers. I do not say white soldiers or Negro soldiers, and I do not say American or British soldiers. To my mind I have had a task in this war that makes me look upon soldiers as soldiers. (As General of the Army, press conference, Paris, France, June 16, 1945).   [767

SOUTH-EAST ASIA TREATY ORGANIZATION

The experience of the United States in the South-East Asia Treaty Organization reaffirms our belief that an international organization of free peoples, conceived in accordance with the principles of the United Nations charter, provides a firm basis for common action to maintain peace and security. (Statement made on Fourth Anniversary of SEATO, Newport, R. I., September 7, 1958).   [768

SPACE AGE

We have just entered upon a scientific age which, in its most fearsome aspects, contains unimaginable threats for civilization. It may be possible that the time will come when the age-old virtues of physical and moral stamina, of courage, of patriotism, and of readiness for self-sacrifice will be meaningless to the nation's preservation. Conceivable—we are told—the day may come when any nation, no matter how small, if guided by perverted thinking, may suddenly unleash upon us or any other, destructive forces against which we would be powerless to defend ourselves. (Speech to American Legion National Commanders, Chicago, Ill., November 20, 1945).   [769

As man-made devices, one after another, have reconoitered the frontiers of space there is a realization that the human race has begun its greatest, most daring adventure. The benefits that will come as man's peaceful conquest of space proceeds should be shared with the world. (QUOTE, February 8, 1959, in first annual space report to Congress).   [770

We shall not be serving mankind well if we become obsessed with just the business of putting new satellites into orbit—so possessed that we overlook the fact that we have some real problems left right here on earth. We need to put new ideas—and more of them—into orbit. (QUOTE, December 6, 1959). [771

All that we have already accomplished, and all in the future that we shall achieve, is the outgrowth not of a soulless, barren technology, nor of a grasping state imperialism. Rather, it is the product of unrestrained human talent and energy and restlessly probing for betterment of humanity. (QUOTE, September 18, 1960, dedicating the George C. Marshall Space Flight Center, Huntsville, Ala.). [772

If you want to send a man to the moon, send a Peace Corps member up there. It is an underdeveloped country. (Speech in Illinois, October, 1961). [773

Anybody who would spend $40 billion in a race to the moon for national prestige is nuts. (QUOTE, July 14, 1963, on Kennedy Administration's space program budget). [774

SPACE EXPLORATION

I believe this thoroughly, and I've said it many times— that we ought to approach scientific explorations into space in a scientific—not a showmanship—way. Let's not take a matter that's purely scientific in its character and in its objectives and make it suddenly a competition with some other nation—or make it a stunt. I don't believe in spectaculars. (Interview, January, 1963). [775

SPACE PROGRAM

Our satellite program has never been conducted as a race with other nations. Rather, it has been carefully scheduled as part of the scientific work of the International Geophysical Year. (News report, Washington, D. C., October 10, 1957). [776

SPIRITUAL TRUTHS

As we build a richer material world, we must always remember that there are spiritual truths which endure forever. They are the universal inspiration of mankind. (Speech to The Associated Press, New York, N. Y., April 25, 1955). [777

STARVATION

Starvation is the implacable foe of social, scientific and political progress. (As Chief of Staff, speech on Veterans' Day, Nebraska State Fair, Lincoln, Nebr., September 1, 1946). [778

STRENGTH

We must not look upon strength as a sin; we must look upon it as a necessity but one only of the contributions we are making to the development of a peaceful world. (As Chief of Staff, Informal Address at Dinner Honoring President Daniel L. Marsh's Twentieth Anniversary at Boston University, Boston, Mass., January 31, 1946). [779

The hand of the aggressor is stayed by strength—and strength alone. (As Supreme Allied Commander in Europe, speech to English Speaking Union, London, England, July 3, 1951). [780

Our economic strength and our military strength are our nation's shields—without which peace could never be preserved, nor freedom defended. All America's acceptance of this basic truth is—in itself—one of America's surest sources of strength. (As Republican Candidate for President, speech at the Alfred E. Smith Memorial Foundation Dinner, New York, N. Y., October 16, 1952). [781

The world thinks of us as a country which is strong, but which will never start a war. (State of the Union Message, Washington, D. C., January 9, 1958). [782

Our strength lies in the diversity of private individuals, organizations, and interests, and in the quality of their technical skills, their imagination, and their initiative. (Speech to Tenth Colombo Plan Meeting, Seattle, Wash., November 10, 1958). [783

... **Helplessness.** There is—in world affairs—a steady course to be followed between an assertion of strength that is truculent and a confession of helplessness that is cowardly. (State of the Union Message, Washington, D. C., February 2, 1953). [784

... **Military; Economic.** Our military strength and our economic strength are truly one. Neither can sensibly be purchased at the price of destroying the other. (Speech to

National Junior Chamber of Commerce, Minneapolis, Minn., June 10, 1953).   [785

... **Spiritual.** I am confident that the American people will see to it that our spiritual strength, that the morale of this country, is just as strong . . . as it was in the days of Lincoln or Washington or the others. (Speech at dedication ceremonies of Eisenhower Presidential Library, Abilene, Kans., May 1, 1962).   [786

SUBVERSION
Scarcely need I assure such an audience as this that I—and my every associate in Government—will keep everlastingly at the job of uprooting subversion wherever it may be found. (Speech to 500 District Leaders of the National Citizens for Eisenhower Congressional Committee, Washington, D. C., June 1954).   [787

SUPREME COURT
The Supreme Court is just as essential to our system of government as is the President or as is the Congress, and we should respect its duties and responsibilities. (News conference, June 26, 1957).   [788

· · T · ·

TAXES

Long-continued taxes that are only a little below the confiscatory level will destroy free government. (Speech to homecoming gathering, Abilene, Kans., May 4, 1952). [789

I believe that taxes are too high . . . It is possible that a few more millions might be squeezed out . . . but certainly, in many instances . . . we have gotten to the point where that individual incentive that has made this nation great is dangerously risked in the process. (As Republican Candidate for President, October, 1952). [790

Our system of taxation must not only provide our Government with the resources to be strong for freedom's sake—but also enable our people to apply their initiative and industry fruitfully. (Speech over radio, Washington, D. C., May 19, 1953). [791

. . . Politics. This matter of taxation is so important to the American people that by no means should it be the subject of political competition. (Speech to Economic Mobilization Conference conducted by the American Management Association, New York City, N. Y., May 20, 1958).   [792

TEACHERS

Good teachers do not just happen. They are the product of the highest personal motivation, encouraged and helped in their work by adequate salaries and the respect, support, good will of their neighbors. (Message on Education sent to Congress, January 12, 1956).   [793

Far more needs to be done in our various communities to enhance the status of the teacher—in salary, in community esteem and support—and thereby attract more people to the profession and, equally important, retain those who bear so well the trust of instructing our youth. (QUOTE, February 3, 1957, urging Congress to vote $1.3 billion over 4 years to help states build new schools).   [794

A good teacher has been defined as an individual who can understand those who are not very good at explaining, and explain to those who are not very good at understanding. (Speech to National Education Association, Washington, D. C., April 4, 1957).   [795

... **Children.** To our teachers we commit the most valuable possessions of the Nation and of the family—our children. (State of the Union Message, Washington, D. C., January 9, 1959).   [796

... **Parents.** I submit that the parent's duty of helping and making a partner of the teacher in the education of his or her child is one of the greatest privileges of free government. (Speech to National Education Association, Washington, D. C., April 4, 1957).   [797

TECHNOLOGY

We now stand in the vestibule of a vast new technological age—one that, despite its capacity for human destruction, has an equal capacity to make poverty and human misery obsolete. If our efforts are wisely directed—and if our unremitting efforts for dependable peace begin to attain some success—we can surely become participants in creating an age characterized by justice and rising levels of human well-being. (State of the Union Message, Washington, D. C., January 7, 1960).   [798

TENSION

We must be prepared during the years ahead to live in a world in which tension and bickering between free nations and the Soviets will be daily experiences. (QUOTE, April 12, 1959, at ceremonies commemorating the 10th Anniversary of NATO).   [799

THANKSGIVING

Let us hope that some day, under a benevolent providence and through the best use of the world's God-given resources, each nation will have reason to celebrate its own Thanksgiving Day. (QUOTE, November 20, 1960, annual Thanksgiving proclamation).   [800

THOUGHT

In every area of political action, free men must think before they can expect to win. (State of the Union Message, Washington, D. C., February 2, 1953).   [801

The need in government is time to think, with the ability of people to do it. (Speech to 12th Annual Washington Conference of the Advertising Council, April 3, 1956). [802

THOUGHT CONTROL

Through knowledge and understanding, we will drive from the temple of freedom all who seek to establish over us thought control—whether they are agents of a foreign state or demagogues thirsty for personal power and public notice. (QUOTE, June 6, 1954, speech at Columbia University, New York, N. Y.). [803

THRIFT

Thrift is one of the characteristics that have made this Nation great. (State of the Union Message, Washington, D. C., January 9, 1959). [804

TIDELANDS OIL

This isn't what I call a fair shake. I call it a shakedown. (QUOTE, October 19, 1952, speech in Texas against government control of tidelands oil). [805

TIME

... **Money.** Frequently time is a more valuable coin than is money. (Speech in Oklahoma City, Okla., November 13, 1957). [806

TOLERANCE

Peace in our society involves more than economic groups; it involves understanding and tolerance among all creeds and races. (As Presidential Nominee of the Republican Party, speech over radio and television, Washington, D. C., September 19, 1956). [807

...**Understanding.** The educator must teach that tolerance is better than a bullet; that understanding is something worthwhile and of far greater value to us than is prejudice; that international differences in the realm of trade and finance and national pride are not so great as to avoid the establishment of, or the addition to, the regimented clusters of white crosses that now stand along the roads of Europe. (As Chief of Staff, Informal address at Dinner Honoring President Daniel L. Marsh's Twentieth Anniversary at Boston University, Boston, Mass., January 31, 1946). [808

TRADE

For our own economic growth we must have continuously expanding world markets; for our security we require that our allies become economically strong. Expanding trade is the only adequate solution for these two present problems confronting our country. (Message to Congress, March 30, 1954). [809

If we fail in our trade policy, we may fail in all. Our domestic employment, our standard of living, our security, and the solidarity of the free world—all are involved. (Message to Congress, March 30, 1954). [810

...**World.** Either we foster flourishing trade between the free nations or we weaken the free world and our own economy. Unless trade links these nations together, our foreign policy will be encased in a sterile vacuum; our domestic economy will shrink within its continental fences. The enlargement of mutually beneficial trade in the free world is an objective to which all of us should be dedicated. (Speech to the Associated Press, New York, N. Y., April 25, 1955).   [811

... **World.**   Strong economic ties are an essential element in our free world partnership. Increasing trade and investment help all of us prosper together. (State of the Union Message, Washington, D. C., January 5, 1956). [812

TRUTH

Never was it more important than it is today that the people of the entire world have free access to the truth. (Speech to The Associated Press, New York, N. Y., April 25, 1955).   [813

... **Simplicity.**   Great truths can, at times, be startingly simple. (As Republican Candidate for President, speech in Milwaukee, Wisc., October 3, 1952).   [814

··U··

UNDERSTANDING

If America is to realize its own destiny in this world of today, we must understand ourselves, but we must also understand others; that it is not enough for universities today merely to say we are training and teaching the young so that twenty years from now they shall be leaders. (As President of Columbia University, speech to The Associated Press, New York, N. Y., April 24, 1950).   [815

A nation's hope of lasting peace cannot be firmly based upon any race in armaments, but rather upon just relations and honest understanding with all other nations. (Speech to American Society of Newspaper Editors, Washington, D. C., April 16, 1953).   [816

We must understand people. We must make it our business to know what they are thinking, and why, and what it means to us. (Speech at Graduation Ceremonies at Foreign Service Institute, June 12, 1959).   [817

...**International.** If this is not to be the age of atomic hysteria and horror, we must make it the age of international understanding and co-operative peace. (Speech to American Newspaper Publishers Association, New York, N. Y., April 22, 1954).   [818

... **International.** International understanding . . . like domestic unity, depends, in large part, on the free, full flow of information and its balanced presentation. (Speech to American Newspaper Publishers Association, New York, N. Y., April 22, 1954).   [819

UNITED NATIONS

In the broader scope, the United Nations, however halting its progress may be, however much its sessions are torn by the jeers and vetoes from one sector, is a viable and working entity—substantial evidence of developing hopes and purposes, an earnest of better things to come. (Speech at Columbia University, New York, N. Y., March 23, 1950).   [820

Never before in history has so much hope for so many people been gathered together in a single organization. Your deliberations and decisions during these somber years have already realized part of those hopes. (Speech to General Assembly of the United Nations, December 8, 1953). [821

That there have been failures in attempts to solve international difficulties by the principles of the Charter, none can deny. That there have been victories, only the willfully blind can fail to see. But clear it is that without the United Nations the failures would still have been written as failures into history and, certainly, without this organization the victories could not have been achieved; instead, they might well have been recorded as human disasters. These, the world has been spared. (Speech to 10th Anniversary Meeting of the United Nations, San Francisco, Calif., June 20, 1955).   [822

As I review the march of world events in recent years I am ever more deeply convinced that the United Nations represents the soundest hope for peace in the world. (Speech over radio and television, Washington, D. C., October 31, 1956).   [823

The United Nations can always be helpful, but it cannot be a wholly dependable protector of freedom when the ambitions of the Soviet Union are involved. (Speech to Congress, Washington, D. C., January 5, 1957).   [824

If the United Nations once admits that international disputes can be settled by using force, then we will have destroyed the very foundation of the organization, and our best hope of establishing a world order. (Speech from the White House, Washington, D. C., February 20, 1957).   [825

There can be no peace in the world unless there is fuller dedication to the basic principles of the United Nations Charter. If ever the United States fails to support these principles the result would be to open the floodgates to direct and indirect aggression throughout the world. (Speech over radio, Washington, D. C., July 15, 1958).   [826

The generating force behind a successful United Nations must be the noble idea that a true international community can build a peace with justice if only people will work together patiently in an atmosphere of open trust. (Speech to Fifteenth General Assembly of the United Nations, New York, N. Y., September 22, 1960).   [827

The problem has always been—in Hiawatha's time as in ours—to channel governments into peaceful ways—to build institutions that make peace easier and war more difficult and eventually impossible. All of us must struggle ceaselessly for the success of the U. N. (Quote, October 23, 1960, speech at Red Wing, Minn.).   [828

. . . Red China. I am completely and unalterably opposed, under the present situation, to the admission of Red China into the United Nations. I personally think that 95 per cent of the population of the United States would take the same stand. (Press conference, July 7, 1954).   [829

UNIVERSAL MILITARY TRAINING

Fairness to the country and to the individual's chances of survival in war demand that each able-bodied citizen receive in time of peace a thorough grounding in technique, discipline and understanding of the citizen's obligations in time of emergency. (Letter to the House Special Committee on Post-War Military Policy, June 2, 1945).   [830

I am told that the purpose of training all our youth, for their own good and for that of the country, is opposed by many of those to whom we have a right to look for spiritual and educational leadership. If this is true, I feel that it must arise from a reluctance to face realities, to study our own history, a history that amply provides the futility of chronic weakness and lack of training in preserving the peace. (Speech to American Legion National Commanders, Chicago, Ill., November 20, 1945).   [831

Universal Military Training is one of the great pillars in the security structure this country must have. (As Chief of Staff, press and radio conference, Washington, D. C., June 27, 1947).   [832

UNIVERSITIES
The whole free world would be stronger if there existed adequate institutions of modern techniques and sciences in areas of the world where the hunger for knowledge and the ability to use knowledge are unsatisfied because educational facilities are not equal to the existing need. (QUOTE, June 3, 1956, accepting honorary degree at Baylor University).   [833

...**Honorary Degrees.** I personally feel that the greatest honor that can come to an individual under the various aspects of our Western civilization is to be awarded an honorary doctorate by one of our great educational institutions. (White House press release, November 19, 1953).   [834

...**Peace.** I was privileged to stay long enough in such a position (as college president) to confirm my belief—my faith—that in the institutions of higher learning, in the secondary and primary schools of this country, there is, almost, our greatest opportunity to help satisfy man's oldest yearning: to live in peace with his fellows. (White House press release, November 19, 1953).   [835

... **Research.** The free university, historically the fountainhead of free ideas and scientific discovery, has experienced a revolution in the conduct of research. Partly because of the huge costs involved, a Government contract becomes virtually a substitute for intellectual curiosity. (Speech over radio and television, Washington, D. C., January 17, 1961).   [836

··V··

VALUES

The world that God has given us is of course material in its values, intellectual and spiritual. We have got to hand all to those who come after us this balance of values and particularly the certainty that they can enjoy the same kind of opportunity in this spiritual, intellectual and material world that we, who will then be their ancestors, enjoyed before them. (Speech to House of Commons, Ottawa, Canada, November 14, 1953).   [837

... **Moral.** The seeds of hate and distrust can be borne on winds that heed no frontier or shore . . . It is my unshakeable belief that only by rejuvenation of respect for moral values can the world possibly come through this long period of tension. (QUOTE, April 19, 1953, commemorating 63rd anniversary of the founding of Pan-American Union).   [838

... **Spiritual.** The ultimate values of mankind are spiritual; these values include liberty, human dignity, opportunity and equal rights and justice. (Speech to AFL–CIO Convention, New York, N. Y., December 5, 1955).   [839

VICE-PRESIDENCY

I believe that it is almost showing indifference to the welfare of the American people unless you keep the Vice President aware of everything that is going on. (Press conference, February 6, 1957).   [840

The role of a Vice President in an Administration is exactly what the President makes it. (Press conference, February 6, 1957).   [841

The Constitution says the Vice President will do certain things. It doesn't say he takes a new oath. It says under certain situations the Vice President does certain things and, when that situation is ended, he doesn't do them any more, and that is the way I see the Constitution. (Press conference, March 5, 1958).   [842

VICTORY

The prerequisite to winning any victory is a single-minded determination to get the job done; a single-minded dedication to that job. Without such determination and dedication there can be no victory but only a stalemate, only a road uphill paced with excuse and evasion. (As Republican Candidate for President, speech in San Francisco, Calif., October 8, 1952).   [843

VIETNAM

The loss of South Vietnam would set in motion a crumbling process that could, as it progresses, have grave consequences for us and for freedom. (Speech at Gettysburg College, Pa., April 4, 1959).   [844

Although the main responsibility for guarding that independence will always, as it has in the past, belong to the Vietnamese people and their government, I want to assure you that for so long as our strength can be useful, the U. S. will continue to assist Vietnam in the difficult yet hopeful struggle ahead. (Message sent to Pres. Ngo Dinh Diem of the Republic of Vietnam on anniversary of independence, October 25, 1960).   [845

I do think, that as long as we have American men fighting and having a great many casualties, we must make Vietnam the priority, ahead of the space program, the war on poverty, everything. (Speech at Republican Dinner, Chicago, Ill., September 30, 1966).   [846

I would not automatically preclude anything. When you appeal to force to carry out the policies of America abroad there is no court above you. (News conference, October 3, 1966).   [847

No one could hope more than I that the President will have a real success in winning the military war (in Vietnam), so that we can give these people in Southeast Asia a better opportunity, better education, a better way of life. (Interview, Gettysburg, Pa., November, 1966).   [848

VOTERS

... **Voting.** Stop shrugging off politics as only the politicians' business; stop banking on American luck to get us good government and good policy—some time it will run out. Stop using the alibi, "one vote doesn't count." It won't, only if not used! And our neighbor's won't, unless we make him use it. (As President of Columbia University, speech to New York Herald Tribune Forum, New York, N. Y., October 25, 1949).   [849

... **Voting.**   Dishonest political promises to selfish groups—not rebuffed at the ballot box—can make a nightmare of the American dream. But wise and determined performance of our civic duties can make that dream come true. (As President of Columbia University, speech to New York Herald Tribune Forum, New York, N. Y., October 25, 1949).   [850

... **Voting.**   Our American heritage is threatened as much by our own indifference as it is by the most unscrupulous office seeker or by the most powerful foreign threat. The future of this Republic is in the hands of the American voter. (As President of Columbia University, speech to New York Herald Tribune Forum, New York, N. Y., October 25, 1949).   [851

... **Voting.**   In the long perspective of history, the right to vote has been one of the strongest pillars of a free society. Our first duty is to protect this right against all encroachment. (State of the Union Message, Washington, D. C., January 7, 1960).   [852

··W··

WAGES

If our economy is to remain healthy, increases in wages and other labor benefits, negotiated by labor and management, must be reasonably related to improvements in productivity. Such increases are beneficial, for they provide wage earners with greater purchasing power. (State of the Union Message, Washington, D. C., January 10, 1957).   [853

All the economic indicators and high-sounding oratory in the world cannot fill the empty place in a pay envelope. (Speech to Republican Women's National Conference, Washington, D. C., March 18, 1958).   [854

WAR

We call war an emergency, and it is just that. Like all emergencies, it usually comes, at least to us, unexpectedly, and from quarters that are not revealed until too late. (Speech to American Legion National Commanders, Chicago, Ill., November 20, 1945).   [855

I hate war as only a soldier who has lived it can, only as one who has seen its brutality, its *stupidity*. Yet there is one thing to say on the credit side—victory required a mighty manifestation of the most ennobling of the virtues of man—faith, courage, fortitude, sacrifice! If we can only hold that example before our eyes; moreover, if we can remember that the international co-operation then so generously displayed points the sure way to the success of the United Nations Organizations, then the war can never be regarded as a total deficit. (Speech to Canadian Club, Ottawa, Canada, January 10, 1946). [856

War . . . has become far more important than a mere clash of armed soldiers. It is the spiritual, intellectual, material, economic, and military might of peoples pitted totally against others; so that lawmakers, policy makers, no longer can say, "Well, we declare war," and then say, "Now, the executives have to carry it out." (As Allied Supreme Commander in Europe, views given to subcommittee of Senate Foreign Relations Committee, Paris, France, July 9, 1951). [857

One great thing about war is that, if and when such a tragedy visits us again, it is always going to happen under circumstances, at places and under conditions different from those you expect or plan for. (Interview, December, 1952). [858

So far as I am concerned, if ever we come to a place that I feel that a step of war is necessary, it is going to be brought about not by any impulsive individualistic act of my own, but I am going before the Congress in the constitutional method set up in this country and lay the problem before them, with my recommendation as to whatever it may be. (Press conference, Washington, D. C., December 2, 1954). [859

The causes of America's wars of this century cannot fairly be laid to any political party or individual. (Speech to Republican National Convention, San Francisco, Calif., July 15, 1964). [860

I do not believe in "gradualism" in fighting a war. I believe in putting in the kind of military strength we need to win, and getting it over with as soon as possible. (Interview, Gettysburg, Pa., November, 1966). [861

... **Brinkmanship.** Now, on this matter of "brinkmanship," the fact of it is, you do have to go to the brink of war to show people that you stand firm; only firmness can keep us out of war. (Interview, January, 1963) . [862

... **Future.** The time approaches . . . when resort to arms may leave the wilderness as the only conqueror. (As Chief of Staff, speech in St. Louis, Mo., February 24, 1947). [863

... **Future.** Whatever the case in the past, war in the future can serve no useful purpose. A war which became general, as any limited action might, could result only in the virtual destruction of mankind. (Speech to the American Society of Newspaper Editors, Washington, D. C., April 21, 1956). [864

... Global. There will be no such thing as a victorious side in any global war of the future. I believe that, any time we begin to think of war as an inescapable event of some future time, that we have become completely pessimistic on the future of humanity, at least in the Northern Hemisphere, as we have known it; and it is really a tragedy that the human imagination and mind won't encompass. (News conference, June 26, 1957).   [865

... Global. In this era of mass-destruction weapons the increasing intimacy in which the peoples of the world live makes resort to global war, even by the smallest of them dangerous to the whole community of nations. (Press release from Taipei, June 18, 1960).   [866

... Ideas. Wars that involve ideas and rights and principles are far more difficult to wage than those that are concerned only with material values. (Speech in Milwaukee, Wisc., October 3, 1952).   [867

... Modern. Modern war does not differentiate between fighting man and helpless child. It combines fortifications and schools and factories into a first priority bomb target. (As Chief of Staff, speech in Edinburgh, Scotland, October 3, 1946).   [868

... Nuclear. In a nuclear war there can be no victors—only losers. (Speech over radio and television, Washington, D. C., May 25, 1960).   [869

... Peace. In discussing war and peace, we incline to paint one all black and the other all white. We like to repeat

"There never was a good war, or a bad peace." But war often has provided the setting for comradeship and understanding and greatness of spirit—among nations, as well as men—beyond anything in quiet days; while peace may be marked by, or may even be the product of chicanery, treachery and the temporary triumph of expediency over all spiritual values. (As President of Columbia University, First of a Series of Lectures Dedicated to the Cause of International Peace, Columbia University, New York, N. Y., April, 1950). [870

... **Peace.** We live in a time when the cost of peace is high. Yet the price of war is higher and is paid in different coin—with the lives of our youth and the devastation of our cities. (Speech over radio and television, Washington, D. C., May 21, 1957). [871

... **Peace.** It is no accident that those who have most intimately lived with the horrors of war are generally the most earnest supporters of these programs to secure peace. (Speech over radio and television, Washington, D. C., May 21, 1957). [872

... **Peace.** As one who has witnessed the horror and the lingering sadness of war, as one who knows that another war could utterly destroy this civilization which has been so slowly and painfully built over thousands of years, I wish I could say tonight that a lasting peace is in sight . . . As a private citizen, I shall never cease to do what little I can to help the world advance along that road. (Speech over radio and television, Washington, D. C., January 17, 1961). [873

...Prevention. The last solution we ever want is war. We don't want war and if we don't want it bad enough, then each of us will do his part to see that it doesn't occur again. (QUOTE, January 23, 1949, as President of Columbia University).   [874

...Preventive. Possibly my hatred of war blinds me so that I cannot comprehend the arguments (the advocates of a preventive war) adduce. But, in my opinion, there is no such thing as a preventive war. Although this suggestion is repeatedly made, none has yet explained how war prevents war. Nor has anyone been able to explain away the fact that war begets conditions that beget further war. (QUOTE, October 21, 1951, as Supreme Commander, North Atlantic Pact Nations).   [875

...Preventive. I think that any reasonable man realizes that there is no such thing as a so-called preventive war. War is war. (Press conference, Paris, France, June, 1952).   [876

...Preventive. When people speak to you about a preventive war, you tell them to go and fight it. After my experience, I have come to hate war. War settles nothing. (QUOTE, April 4, 1965).   [877

WARFARE

The history of warfare is a constant evolution, with changing weapons and tactics. We are living in a period when the trend moves forward at an accelerated pace. No man can picture accurately, today, the face or appearance of a possible war in 1967. The outlines, the possibilities, the definite requirements of the present that stand forth with reasonable clarity, take on increasing haziness the further we attempt to project them against the future. We must avoid stagnation, rigid dogma, complacency; until the need for armaments shall pass, we must be certain that ours are suited to the possibility of their day. (Speech to American Legion, New York, N. Y., August 29, 1947). [878

... **Ideological.** The struggle going on in the world is for the minds and hearts of men. It is an ideological struggle. There is every possible way of going about the thing, and open warfare is only one method. (QUOTE, September 9, 1951, as Supreme Commander, North Atlantic Pact Nations). [879

... **Psychological.** While we have been dozing at the gate of the psychological, strategists of Communism have crept into our citadel. (As Republican Candidate for President, speech in San Francisco, Calif., October 8, 1952). [880

WATER

So crucial to our future has water become, that I have assigned appropriate surveys and plans concerning it to a special committee of the Cabinet, and to the Hoover Commission as well. These studies, when subjected to Congressional action, will undoubtedly result in the comprehensive water policy that this country has needed since its very beginning. (Speech at dedication of McNary Dam, Ore., September 23, 1954). [881

The whole matter of making the best use of each drop of water from the moment it touches our soil until it reaches the oceans, for such purposes as irrigation, flood control, power production, and domestic and industrial uses clearly demands the closest kind of cooperation and partnership between municipalities, States, and the Federal Government . . . Until such partnership is established on a proper and logical basis of sharing authority, responsibility, and costs, our country will never have both the fully productive use of water that it so obviously needs and protection against disastrous floods. (State of the Union Message, Washington, D. C., January 10, 1957).   [882

. . . Conservation. Among these treasures of our land is water—fast becoming our most valuable, most prized, most critical resource. A blessing when properly used—but it can bring devastation and ruin when left uncontrolled. It is, therefore, essential that every drop of water, from the moment that it falls upon our land, be turned to the service of our people. (Speech at dedication of McNary Dam, Ore., September 23, 1954).   [883

WHITE HOUSE, THE
The White House is too much a symbol . . . to most Americans . . . to be abandoned as the residence of the Chief Executive. (QUOTE, March 17, 1957, on the proposal to build a new mansion and turn the White House into a museum).   [884

WISDOM
. . . Political. All political wisdom does not reside in the White House, nor in the executive branch, nor in Washing-

ton itself. (QUOTE, May 10, 1953, greeting state and territorial governors).   [885

WORDS

. . . **Deeds.** We cannot salute the future with bold words
while we surrender it with feeble deeds. (As Republican
Nominee for President, speech over radio and television,
Washington, D. C., September 19, 1956).   [886

WORK

How are you going to get ahead in the world? By hard
work—that was always the American way. But now, no
longer do our people take pride in good work well done.
(Interview, Gettysburg, Pa., November, 1966).   [887

WORKERS

. . . **Age.** Many workers in our country are denied re-
warding employment merely because they happen to be over
45 years of age. This arbitrary bar . . . causes a waste of
valuable skills and talents and must be eliminated. (QUOTE,
September 11, 1955).   [888

WORLD

. . . **Affairs.** Unless we look, with clear and understanding eyes at the world situation confronting us and meet with
dynamic purposes the issues, contained therein, then we will
lose the American birthright. The system of government
established by our forefathers will disappear. The American
record, from Washington to the day of that disaster, will be
only a blank page in history. (As President of Columbia

University, speech at opening of Crusade for Freedom, Denver, Colo., September 4, 1950).   [889

... Betterment. We are striving to make a better world for ourselves, for our children, that kind of world in which free men can live—and I think it is just that simple and just that important. As long as we approach it in that way, I think we shall never give up. On the contrary, I think we shall win. (Speech to Members of the Committee for a National Trade Policy, Washington, D. C., June 14, 1957).   [890

... Community. The nature of today's weapons, the nature of modern communications, and the widening circle of new nations make it plain that we must, in the end, be a world community of open societies. (Speech to United Nations General Assembly, New York, N. Y., August 13, 1958).   [891

... Cooperation. We live in a small world, and only by a cooperative effort of the free peoples occupying important areas can we build security and peace. (Speech to American Newspaper Publishers Association, New York, N. Y., April 22, 1954).   [892

... Governments. If there is room in our own country for every shade of political and social and religious thinking and expression, there is room in the world for different philosophies of government, so long as none is dedicated to the forceful imposition of its political creed on others.

(Speech to New York Herald Tribune Forum, New York, N. Y., October 30, 1946). [893

. . . Health. The world cups its ears to hear the rattling of rockets. It listens less closely to the sound of peace and well-being which emanate from the slow but steady improvement in the world health and nutrition. (Speech to Fifth International Congress on Nutrition, Washington, D. C., September 1, 1960). [894

. . . Relations. Our own national life will be the healthier, make no mistake about it; if we abide by the principles of democracy in our relations with other peoples, we shall strengthen them at home; the wider their exercise, the more firm their case. (As Chief of Staff, speech at Wings Club, New York, N. Y., May 5, 1947). [895

. . . Relations. In our relations with other nations, our attitude will reflect full recognition of their sovereign and equal status. We shall deal with common problems in a spirit of partnership. (Speech to United Nations, San Francisco, Calif., June 20, 1955). [896

. . . Trade. America is today the world's greatest trading nation. If we use this great asset wisely to meet the expanding demands of the world, we shall not only provide future opportunities for our own business, agriculture and labor, but in the process strengthen our security posture and other prospects for a prosperous, harmonious world. (State of the Union Message, Washington, D. C., January 9, 1958). [897

... Trade. World trade helps to lay the groundwork for peace by making all free nations of the world stronger and more self-reliant. (State of the Union Message, Washington, D. C., January 9, 1958). [898

... Trade. For many of the less developed countries, export trade is concentrated in a few primary commodities. To maintain a healthy world demand for these commodities, we must have a high and expanding level of economic activity throughout the free world. (Speech to Tenth Colombo Plan Meeting, Seattle, Wash., November 10, 1958). [899

... Unity. No free people can for long cling to any privilege or enjoy any safety in economic solitude. For all our own material might, even we need markets in the world for the surpluses of our farms and our factories. . . . So we are persuaded by necessity and by belief that the strength of all free peoples lies in unity; their danger, in discord. (First Inaugural Address, January 20, 1953). [900

WORLD WAR II

More than any other war in history, this war has been an array of the forces of evil against those of righteousness. It had to have its leaders and it had to be won—but no matter what the sacrifice, no matter what the suffering of populations, no matter what the cost, the war had to be won. (As General of the Army, speech on receiving the Order of Victory from Marshal Gregory K. Zhukov, Frankfort-on-the-Main, Germany, June 10, 1945). [901

... V-E Day. I think May 8th represented for a great many people in Europe at that time practically the realization of all their dreams and, you might say, their ambitions. Certainly I thought it marked for me, you might say, the end of an active career. I saw a nice farm over the other side of the ocean—and it still is a long ways away at least. (Press conference, April 27, 1955). [902

WORLD WAR III

The only way to win World War III is to prevent it. (As Republican Nominee for President, speech over radio and television, Washington, D. C., September 19, 1956). [903

··Y··

YOUTH

I have been fortunate that my own life has been spent with America's young people. The grave decisions that I have been compelled to make, at least before this calendar year, have been vindicated by the skill, the sense of responsibility and the sacrifice of America's young men. My faith in them is my unbounded faith in America itself. (Speech to National Junior Chamber of Commerce, Minneapolis, Minn., June 10, 1953).   [904

People come in and want my views. I'm particularly encouraged by the attractiveness and personality of the young people who come to see me. (News conference, Gettysburg, Pa., November 7, 1966).   [905

...Demonstrations. I think some young people feel they have to demonstrate, wear their hair long and call attention to themselves because they are suffering from an inferiority complex. They have to make themselves seen and heard in some way. They are gaining headlines—but they are creating an image of American youth that is false. (News conference, Gettysburg, Pa., November 7, 1966).   [906

... **Rebellion.** The spirit of rebellion is rather healthy in young people. But rebellion must accept the guidelines of civilization—honesty, decency, monogamy, virtue in sexual relations. (News conference Gettysburg, Pa., November 7, 1966). ⸴ [907

Biographical Sketch

DWIGHT DAVID EISENHOWER

BORN	October 14, 1890 Denison, Texas.
PARENTS	David and Ida Elizabeth Stover Eisenhower
MARRIED	Mamie Geneva Doud, 1916
EDUCATION	Graduated from high school 1909 U S Military Academy at West Point 1911–1915.

VOCATION	1915	Assigned as 2nd Lieutenant to Fort Sam Houston in San Antonio, Texas.
	1918	Placed in command of Camp Colt, Gettysburg, Pa., a tank training center.
	1933–35	Assigned to office of Chief of Staff under Gen. Douglas MacArthur.
	1935–39	Member of American Military Mission to The Philippines, where he helped develop a Philippine defense plan, found

	a military academy and organize, train and equip the first Philippine army and reserve force.
1939	Returned to U S and became executive officer of 15th Infantry Division.
1940	Named chief of staff of Third Division with headquarters at Fort Lewison.
1941	Promoted to Brigadier-General stationed at San Antonio.
1942	Chief of War Plans Division, U. S. General Staff.
1942	Commander-in-Chief of U. S. Forces in European theater; Commander of Allied Forces in N. W. Africa.
1943	Attended Cairo Conference of Pres. Franklin D. Roosevelt, Prime Minister Winston Churchill and Chiang Kai-shek.
1943–45	Commander in Chief Allied Expeditionary Forces in Western Europe.
1944	Promoted to General.
1945–48	Chief of Staff U. S. Army.
1948–53	President of Columbia University.
1951–52	Commander of newly-established Supreme Headquarters, Allied Powers in Europe (SHAPE).
1953–61	34th President of the United States of America.

1948   *Crusade in Europe.*

Distinguished Service Medal 1928

Oak Leaf Cluster to Distinguished Service
    Medal for plan and execution of North
    African Campaign—W. W. II.

Second Oak Leaf Cluster for service as Gen-
    eral of the Army during operations in
    Western Europe—W. W. II.

Distinguished Service Medal (Navy).

Legion of Merit.

Freedom of the cities of Edinburgh, Scot-
    land; Belfast, Ireland and London, Eng-
    land, and the Burgh of Regality of May-
    bole, Scotland; Swords of Honor of the
    City of London and of the Netherlands;
    gold medals of the City of Amsterdam,
    Holland; Rheims, France, and the City of
    New York.

Bronze Award, Freedom House, New York
    City.

Medal of Honor, Roosevelt Memorial Associ-
    ation.

Churchman Award.

Army and Navy Union Medal.

Poor Richard Club Medal.

Pennsylvania Society of New York Gold
    Medal.

Catholic War Veterans Certificate of Merit.

American Hebrew Medal of 1945.

231

Gen. Sylvanus Thayer Gold Medal and Scroll West Point 1961.

First American Patriots Medal Freedoms Foundation 1961.

General Eisenhower has been honored by the award of memberships in both military and civil orders of numerous countries in both hemispheres, including:

Knight Grand Cross of the Order of the Bath and the Order of Merit of Great Britain

Grand Cross of the Legion of Honor and Croix de Guerre with Palms of France.

CHILDREN   Doud Dwight 1917 (died in childhood).

John Sheldon Doud 1922

RESIDENCE   Gettysburg, Pa.

MUSEUM   In Abilene, Kans. has been established the Eisenhower Museum and Home by the Eisenhower Foundation to Promote Citizenship and to Honor Veterans of America's Wars, and here are preserved the General's trophies and medals.

Index

236

About the Editor

Elsie Gollagher, a native of Welbourn, Lincolnshire, England, is Editor of QUOTE Magazine and a Senior Book Editor of Droke House Publishers.

From 1939 to 1946 she served with the British Civil Service, and in 1947 joined the staff of QUOTE Magazine in Indianapolis, Indiana.

Mrs. Gollagher is now an American citizen, married to Charles K. Gollagher and residing in Plainfield, Indiana.

Quote

THE QUOTABLE DWIGHT D. EISENHOWER is one of six volumes of the quotations of America's foremost living political figures. The series, published by Droke House, includes: THE QUOTABLE HARRY S. TRUMAN, HUBERT H. HUMPHREY, ROBERT F. KENNEDY, RICHARD M. NIXON AND LYNDON B. JOHNSON.

Each book contains 750 to 1,000 quotations showing in his own words, where each of these political leaders stands on the important issues of today—as well as where he has stood in the past.

For the first time, here are complete reference works on the positions, ideas and comments of every leading presidential aspirant, as well as the incumbent president and two living former presidents. Each volume is completely indexed and contains a biographical sketch.

For 27 years, QUOTE, The Weekly Digest for public speakers has recorded a history of the times in the words of the men and women making that history. As a continuing service, the staff of QUOTE has worked with outstanding editors on this current series of political books.